Suzannah Olivier is a qualified nutritionist, writes health features for a wide variety of publications and has published several books on health matters.

Also by Suzannah Olivier

What Should I Feed My Baby?
The Breast Cancer Prevention and Recovery Diet
The Stress Protection Plan
101 Ways to Simplify Your Life
500 of the Most Important Stress-Busting Tips You'll Ever Need

The *You Are What You Eat* series:
Banish Bloating
Maximising Energy
Natural Hormone Balance
Eating for a Perfect Pregnancy
Allergy Solutions
The Detox Manual

HEALTHY FOOD FOR HAPPY KIDS

an a–z of nutritional know-how

Suzannah Olivier

SIMON & SCHUSTER

LONDON • NEW YORK • SYDNEY • TOKYO • TORONTO • DUBLIN

A VIACOM COMPANY

First published in Great Britain by Simon & Schuster, 2004
A Viacom Company

Copyright © Suzannah Olivier, 2004

1 3 5 7 9 10 8 6 4 2

Simon & Schuster UK Ltd
Africa House
64–78 Kingsway
London WC2B 6AH

www.simonsays.co.uk

Simon & Schuster Australia
Sydney

A CIP catalogue record for this book is available from the British Library

ISBN 0-7432-4810-4

This publication contains the opinions and ideas of its author. It is intended to
provide helpful and informative material on the subjects addressed in the
publication. It is sold with the understanding that the author and publisher are
not engaged in rendering medical, health, or any other kind of personal professional services in the book. The reader should consult his or her medical,
health or other competent professional before adopting any of the suggestions in
this book or drawing inferences from it. The author and publisher specifically
disclaim all responsibility for any liability, loss or risk, personal or otherwise,
which is incurred as a consequence, directly or indirectly, of the use and
application of any of the contents of this book.

Typeset by Palimpsest Book Production Limited, Polmont, Stirlingshire
Printed and bound in Great Britain by
Mackays of Chatham Ltd, Chatham, Kent

Contents

Introduction

Healthy Food for
Happy Kids   1

A

Advertising Whoppers   4
Appetite Squashers   10

B

Balancing the Diet Books   13
Best Behaviour and
Concentration   18
Boost the Nutrient Value
of Meals   22
Brain Food   24
Breakfast   27
Busy Parents   30

C

Childminders   33
Choice   35
Convenience Food –
Healthier Options   37

D

Desserts   42
Diabetes   47
Disordered Eating   49
Drink to Health   51

E

Electronic Nanny   57
Energy   59
Exercise and Sport   61

F

Faddy Eating   63
Family Mealtimes   65
Fast Food   68
Food as Medicine   71
Asthma   72
Ear Infections   76
Eczema   77
Hay Fever   79
Headaches   80
Food Intolerances   82
Fruit and Vegetables   87

G

Good Food Fun   93
Growth and Height   95

H

Holiday Eating   99
Home Remedy Kit   102

I

Immune Boost   107

J

Junk Food 116

K

Kids in the Kitchen 121
Kitchen Hygiene 125
Kitchen Shortcuts 126

L

Labels I – Deciphering Them 128
Labels II – Additives 134
Learning About Food 138
Learning Difficulties 142
Lunchbox Planning 147
Lunchbox Questions 160

M

Milk and Dairy 162
Munchies 169

N

Nutrition Needs 172

O

Obesity 177
Organic Eating 181
Outdoor Eating 187

P

Parent Power 191
Party Time 193
Peanut and Other Allergies 195
Pester Power and
    Peer Pressure 204
Projects and Activities 207

Q

Questions 210

R

Restaurants 211

S

Salt Sellers 213
School Catering 218
Seasonal Eating 221
Slow Food 222
Store Cupboard Standbys 223
Sugar 225
Sweeteners 228

T

Tens and Teens 232
Toddlers and Food
    Independence 235
Toothy Issues 236
Tummy Trouble and Toilet 240
    Problems

V

Vegetarians and Vegans 246
Vitamins and Minerals 251

W

Water 270
Wet Beds 272

X

X-tra Insurance –
    Supplements 274

Y

Young Helpers 277

Z

Zzzzzzz . . . 279

Solutions for Meal Planning

Breakfast Ideas	see Breakfast	page 27
Quick Main Meals	see Busy Parents	page 30
Home Versions of Children's Favourites	see Convenience Foods – Healthier Options	page 37
Ideas for Kids Cookery	see Kids in the Kitchen	page 121
Healthy, Yummy Desserts	see Desserts	page 42
Delicious Drinks	see Drink to Health	page 51
Food for All the Family	see Family Mealtimes	page 65
Serving Ideas for Fruits and Vegetables	see Fruits and Vegetables	page 87
Healthy Snack Ideas	see Munchies	page 169
Wheat- and Dairy-Free Baking Recipes	see Food Intolerances	page 82
Sandwich Filling Suggestions	see Lunchbox Planning	page 147
Lunchbox Planner	see Lunchbox Planning	page 147
Picnic and Barbecue Ideas	see Outdoor Eating	page 187
Birthday Party Plans	see Party Time	page 193
Emergency Meals	see Store Cupboard Standbys	page 223

Introduction

In order to be reading even this far, you must care about the food your child is eating. You will know that establishing the foundations of excellent health is one of the greatest gifts you can give your child and one of the most lasting ways to do this is through good food. Whether you are a parent or grandparent, a teacher or childminder, I hope you find the information in this book will serve you well. Eating nutritious food will help your child to have even moods, concentrate, do well at school, and resist illness.

Some of the most important health messages aimed at child health – eating five portions of fruit and vegetables daily, avoiding 'chips with everything', and the detrimental effect of sugar on young teeth – are slowly beginning to permeate the nation's consciousness. However there still remain huge gaps. Parents undoubtedly want to do the best for their children, but are faced with confusing information, often do not have the time to cook from scratch, and are worn down by the effects of pester power.

The question that parents ask me most frequently is no longer 'Why?', but 'How?'. How do I get my child to eat up? How can I encourage my child to eat vegetables? How do I plan a varied diet? How do I steer my child away from overdosing on sugary sweets?

The good news is that it isn't really that complicated. It does, however, involve a degree of consistency and determination, some time and a hefty dose of common sense. And having children often provides the motivation needed to slow down and attend to the basics, such as cooking fresh food and eating as a family. Obviously the earlier you can help your children to establish good habits the easier it is. Children are easily waylaid by any number of health-demolishing habits, including fast-food, heavily advertised kid's food and sedentary activities.

The '64 million dollar' question really should be 'Why do we – as a society and as individuals – give our children the worst possible food available?' Because that is what most processed foods are, and there is no doubt that this is affecting their health. Recent alarming headlines in the press have highlighted the problem:

- Children's diet was better in the 1950s.
- Families fight over food fads.
- Children eat up £365m between home and school.
- Food firms to blame for children's high salt intake.
- Fat children may die before their parents.

What is a parent to do? Well, if you have a gut feeling that something has to give, and that something is the food choices made on a daily basis, then you are 50 per cent there already. Education is key. A major theme throughout this book is that of involving your child in the process of choosing and preparing foods. Only by educating our children to enjoy real food and to be knowledgeable about the effects of food choices on health can we hope to make a difference for the long term. It is really an investment for the future. But it is also fun! What a joy to see a child selecting different foods, savouring them, enjoying eating at the table and, even better, rolling sleeves up and getting stuck in to chopping, stirring and tasting. Above all, and despite the serious intent, I hope you all enjoy yourselves implementing the information contained in this book.

Arranged as an A–Z so you can instantly access the section you need, this book is designed to give to-the-point answers for busy parents. Each section is cross-referenced to others to give further information. Most give handy hints, tips and check lists, as well as website addresses for digging deeper. In addition to providing ideas to help you and your children to learn about, appreciate and eat good food, there are also sections dealing with the major diet-linked childhood health issues, plus strategies to help make changes for the better.

For more tips, games and ideas of how to put theory into practice, visit www.HealthyFood4HappyKids.com

Advertising Whoppers

Advertising aimed specifically at kids is a real pain for parents, but there are ways that it can be used to help teach children about the realities of our commercial world and there are ways of fighting back – it is not all hopeless! The first bit of this section takes the form of a bit of a rant, but before you pass it over it does help to be aware of the issues.

Advertising aimed at children takes may forms, many of which are insidious. Straightforward TV advertising and the promotion of products with cartoon characters are bad enough (there could be whole cartoon feature films playing out in chill cabinets), but parents also have to fend off pester power resulting from clever 'product placement', product endorsement by sports and music personalities, internet marketing and school sponsoring schemes. Shockingly, advertisers even collect personal data from children enabling them to be even more targeted with specific mailings.

TV and radio advertising to kids is (supposedly) regulated, but advertisers have become very adept at circumventing this. For example, sub-teenagers – or tweenies – now form a major sector of TV soap opera audiences. As these programmes are broadcast outside of the children's TV bracket there are fewer restrictions on the advertisements placed during these programmes – and advertising agencies capitalise on this. Even where advertising to kids on TV is regulated, it really only pays lip-service to the concerns of many parents. Non-broadcast advertising, such as in magazines and on billboards, is covered by industry-wide, self-regulatory guidelines. Internet advertising is not regulated at all, other than what the search engines manage to impose, which is precious little.

In Sweden, they are much more strict and have taken the bold step of simply banning advertising to kids under 12 years of age, across the board. We have not yet been brave enough to do this – even though UK children aged four to nine watch an average of a worrying 2.5 hours of TV and videos each day – and our children's health is suffering as a result.

A report from Sustain (TV Dinners – what's being served up by the advertisers? www.sustainweb.org) has shown that the amount of money spent on advertising foods on TV to children is directly inverse to the health qualities of the food. A negligible amount of food advertising budgets is spent on fruit, vegetables, potatoes or bread, which needless to say have limited profit margins, whereas 99 per cent is spent on questionable products such as sugary breakfast cereals, sweets, crisps and soft drinks – foods that are high in sugar, salt and fat, but which also have high profit margins. This means that your child has to sort the conflicting messages being advertised on TV against the healthy eating messages. Not easy!

One of the most appalling trends is the encroachment of advertising to captive school children within the school environment – aided and abetted by the schools themselves. These take the form of collectable coupons to buy school equipment, sponsorship of all sorts of school facilities from notebooks to sporting endeavours to whole canteens, as well as drink machines deliberately placed to crowd out other options such as milk drinks. The most recent move in the US, which we could all too easily follow, is the implementation of a sales target that amounts to each child buying a can of cola-type drink from these machines in order to maintain the school's financial income from these companies.

In the ad-executives' eyes, your child is a customer from the womb onwards and brand loyalty is established in a child from as young as two years of age. Large conferences are regularly run on subjects such as 'Marketing to Pre-school Kids and Parents', with speakers who include, for example, child psychologists and experts from a certain publicly funded, non-commercial TV station. I wonder if these people have children themselves and if they sleep at night?

What Can Parents Do?

In the face of all of this, what can a parent do about the influence of food-related advertising? In truth, advertising is everywhere and this is unlikely to change in the foreseeable future, so realistically you have to teach your children to become critical consumers. If you remain consistent in your approach it does eventually make a difference, though on occasions you will need an iron will.

Start Young

- All babies are born with stone-age instincts and tastes. They do not automatically crave large amounts of salty, sugary or fatty foods. The earlier you establish a taste for good food the easier it will be. In fact, recently, some children who worked on cocoa plantations and had a very simple diet, were given chocolate – the end product of their labours – to taste and they found it unbearably sweet.

- Children are influenced by their parents' shopping behaviour. If they see you impulse buying and not working out the pros and cons of purchases then they will follow suit.

Why Whining Works

- Toddlers typically use an irritating whine when they want something and don't stop until they succeed. Given that they have little control over their environment, repeated whining is an understandable strategy. But it still wears parents down. As your child gets older, teach him not to whine, but to ask 'normally', and discuss the pros and cons of a purchase. Tell your child that the reward is that you might occasionally say 'yes' to a well-reasoned argument against a flat 'no' to a whine.

Becoming a Critical Consumer

- Examine how you shop. Do you budget? Are you an impulse buyer? Do you discuss value for money with your children? Which products do you treat as luxuries? Do you regularly use prepared, packaged foods? Now ask yourself, how are your habits influencing your children?
- Offer opinions about products. Is it useful or not? Is it well made or a piece of fall-apart-junk? Is it costly or does it offer good value? Is it clever or ridiculous?
- Explain that products do not always live up to their claims. This does not have to be all serious and boring talk. For instance, you could invent a detective game. Your child is Detective Catch'em-at-it on the trail of Lies and Half-Truths. See how many eye-stretching whoppers he or she can find on TV and on food packaging, and keep a detective notebook-log.

Understanding How Advertising Works

- Start with understanding the difference between an advert, a fantasy programme/character and real life. Children cannot always differentiate and you need to point out 'This is a commercial, the programme will carry on afterwards'. Talk to them about how animation is made, how cows are made to look as if they are dancing, and why an ice cream can do somersaults off the wall. Explain to them how these tactics and humour help to make a product more appealing.

- Many children's adverts appeal to the devil of instant gratification. By avoiding impulse purchases and having structured buying times, say an outing to spend pocket money once a week, you can begin to instil a more measured approach.

Budgeting and Value

- Value is a difficult concept to get across to a child, but simply saying 'We don't have enough money to buy this today' initially, while showing her an empty wallet, is a good place to start. As your child gets older you can explain 'If I buy this now then I will not have enough money to take you to the cinema/ swimming/roller blading later today'.

- Point out that the reason companies advertise is that there are huge profit margins in the worst of products (50–300 per cent for something laden with sugar and colouring, against 20 per cent for some fresh produce).

- Point out that products using certain endorsements, such as film, cartoon or sporting characters, are often much more expensive than the same product without this promotion. Link it to their pocket money, if you can.

Divert Attention

- Instead of encouraging brand loyalty to foodstuffs, by joining clubs or collecting coupons, divert your child towards brand loyalty clubs for toys that offer some lasting value – log on to websites with building ideas or creative modelling (such as Lego or K'Nex). They get the same thrill.
- Children like small novelty foods such as squeezy tubes. Create your own novelty foods by cutting things into fun shapes or making faces with food, and stock up with small 'give-aways' to fend off the collectable toy items available with many meals.

You Have the Ultimate Veto

- You can always refuse to buy a product. Your child's anger and frustration will only last a short while and it will quickly be forgotten, yet an important principle will have been strengthened – in other words, a little bit of short-term pain in the interest of long-term gain.
- Limit their exposure. You can also avoid cable TV, block certain types of internet sites and prevent them having their own TV set.

Use Influence Where You Can

- Talk to your child's school and team up with other parents if you are concerned about the messages being broadcast to your children by product placement and vending machines in school buildings (*see* Parent Power, page 191).

Speak the Language Your Children Speak

- Ad-execs spend a lot of time dreaming up words that appeal to kid's, such as 'noodle-tastic', 'bonkers' flavours and the words 'wicked orange' instead of tartrazine colouring. Interestingly, the tactics employed by the advertising industry can also be used to advantage. Important research from the Psychology Department at Bangor University found that when advertising tactics were employed to encourage children to eat fruit and vegetables they had an astounding success rate. Heroic cartoon characters, The Food Dudes, were used, who fought off the force of evil (The Junk Food Junta) and shouted 'If I eat my fruit tonight, General Junk will get a fright'. This was linked to a reward scheme with small items such as Food Dude pencils, caps, T-shirts and lunchboxes. Intake for both fruits and vegetables were doubled or even tripled and the effects were long lasting – when revisted more than a year later consumption was still at the upper end or even higher. For more on this visit www.fooddudes.co.uk

- For a copy of *Parent Power: Raising Children in a Commercial World*, look at www.fau.org.uk or contact the Food Advertising Unit (Advertising Association) 020 7828 2771.

See also Pester Power and Peer Pressure, page 204.

Appetite Squashers

How often do you tell your child 'Eat up or you won't grow big and strong' or 'Finish all your food, think about the poor children in . . . (insert the name of whichever poor, war-torn region is in the news at the moment). And as you repeat these mantras, recall how your parents would say precisely the same things to you. And did it work? Of course not. We get very emotional about whether our children are eating up their food or not. It is the natural desire of parents for their children to be well fed, and parents worry if children do not seem to be eating properly. And yet, to quote another cliché, you don't see children who endure a shortage of food, in some of those countries we see on the nightly news, refusing food. The oversupply of food and choice has skewed, somewhat, our perception of appetite, nutrition and children's eating habits.

Children's appetites can go in fits and starts. Just because they eat less for a while does not necessarily mean that anything is wrong. Usually their appetite will adjust again just before a growth spurt. Of course, if poor appetite goes on for too long then you should consult your doctor or health visitor. If your child is continuing to put on weight and is growing then there is unlikely to be any cause for concern.

Children also often temporarily lose their appetite when they are under the weather or ill. They might even lose a little weight when this happens. As long as this is short-term there is no need for concern.

In such situations, children react instinctively and their bodies divert their energy resources away from the business of digestion into immune defences. Forcing them to eat at this time, if they do not wish to, is counterproductive. The main thing is to maintain their liquid intake with water, fruit juices, thin soups and smoothies. If you are in any doubt, consult your doctor.

What Can You Do?

- Small children don't necessarily have an appetite for large meals. It may suit them better to eat five or six small, snack-sized meals a day instead of three main meals. This does not mean that they should eat snacks on the run five times daily – it just means serving them smaller portions at meal times and giving them healthy snacks.
- Children are often overwhelmed by too much food on their

plates. Serve small portions – they can always have second helpings if they are still hungry.

- If your child has not eaten his meal, only offer nutritious snacks
  later on, instead of fillers such as crisps or biscuits.

- If your child seems to have a poor appetite, it may be worth
  examining other things you are doing. Is your child distracted
  at the table, for instance? Sometimes it is best to just concentrate on eating instead of playing games or providing toys or TV.

- Are you reading the signals properly? Children might not say
  they are hungry but just get irritable. Erratic behaviour may
  mean that they need more regular meal times.

- Ask yourself if you are giving them the ammunition for using
  food as a emotional tool. If they know that you get upset if the
  plate is not wiped clean then this can become a battleground.
  If you don't let it worry you, the chances are that your child
  will let go of this way of getting to you and will eat up at subsequent meals, as long as you are consistent.

- Juices, squashes, colas and sodas are full of appetite-blunting
  sugar, and if your child is consuming these you must substitute
  water. Sweets have a similar effect.

- Milk between meals also blunts appetite. It is obviously a
  source of calcium and other nutrients, but milk is really a
  food and not a drink and so it is no surprise if a child who
  frequently drinks milk between meals is not very hungry. If
  you want your child to get nutrients from a wider variety of
  foods it may be best to reduce the amount of milk drunk by
  half. Their appetite for other foods should then increase. An
  over-reliance on milk as a source of nutrition is a common
  reason for iron deficiency (which is the most widespread
  nutritional deficiency in children).

See also Disordered Eating, page 49, and Growth and Height,
page 95.

Balancing the Diet Books

The term 'a balanced diet' seems to mean different things to different people, and many parents remain totally confused. To some, a balanced diet means eating more fruit and vegetables, to others it means eating more 'good' food and less 'bad' food, and to yet others it means some nutritionally ideal utopia which they are unlikely to achieve and so might as well not bother!

As far as children are concerned, it is a simple fact that the majority of children are not getting this mysteriously elusive balanced diet, maybe, amongst other reasons, precisely because their parents are unsure of what it really means. The best practical interpretation of a balanced diet that I can come up with, which is useful to parents, is to ensure your child is eating a varied diet. By eating a variety of foods from as wide a choice as possible, across the food groups, your child is likely to get the most nutritionally complete balance.

What Are Today's Children Eating?

We have a very clear idea about this, thanks to The National Diet and Nutrition Surveys of Children aged 1.5–4.5 years old and 4–18 years old. But the picture is not an encouraging one. What these surveys tell us is that the average child is neither getting a balanced diet, nor adequate intakes of important nutrients. The general findings are that:

- The most commonly eaten foods, consumed by over 80 per cent of children, are white bread, crisps, biscuits, potatoes and chocolate bars.
- Nearly two-thirds eat no green leafy vegetables at all. Only a quarter of children eat raw vegetables (such as carrot sticks or tomatoes) or salad.
- The average child eats only two portions of fruit and vegetables daily, against the recommended minimum of five portions. One-fifth of children do not eat fruit at all.
- Children eat twice the amount of salt that is recommended.
- Most children eat too much saturated fat and too much sugar. No recommendations exist for fibre, but it was noted that children who consumed more dietary fibre also experienced less constipation.
- Just over one-third eat fish, but most of this was fish fingers or fish and chips – only one in ten eats plain white fish and one in six eats oily fish.
- Deficiencies abound. Here are a couple of typical sets of findings in two of the represented age groups:

  - In children aged 1.5–4.5 years, half consumed less than the RNI (reference nutrient intake) for vitamin A, 95 per cent got less than the RNI for vitamin D, 84 per cent were low in iron and 72 per cent were low in zinc.

— In 11–14-year-old girls when pitched against the LRNI (lower reference nutrient intake), which really is the lowest of low amongst standards, 45 per cent were low in iron, 51 per cent were low in magnesium, 37 per cent were low in zinc, 15 per cent were low in potassium, 24 per cent were low in calcium, 20 per cent were low in vitamin A and 22 per cent were low in vitamin B_2. Boys' intakes in this age group were about 50 per cent better for each figure, but remember this is the LRNIs, which are pretty poor levels anyway.

So how did these children, who are a fair representation of most of the children in the UK, arrive at this sorry state? The likelihood is that they are victims of what I call 'the three kids' mealtime madnesses':

- They eat special 'kids' foods' – which, incidentally, are the worst of all types of processed foods.
- They choose, and more to the point are offered, a limited variety of foods with restricted flavours and textures.
- The chances are that they often eat separately from their parents, which limits their food education horizons.

So What Does Balance Mean?

To combat this uncertainty the Balance of Good Health plate was designed by the Health Education Authority. The plate is divided into thirds:

- One-third represents fruits and vegetables.
- One-third represents grains and starches (i.e. bread, pasta, rice).
- The remaining third is divided mainly between protein foods, such as meat or meat substitutes, and dairy and cheese products (or,

as I prefer to put it, calcium-rich foods), with a smaller tranche 'permitted' for oils, fats, sugar and sugary foods.

This visual tool is quite helpful when looking at the overall balance of a meal and it is easy to see where improvements can be made. If you are looking at a plate of food and it is mainly starchy foods and meat – say a bacon sandwich – then it is easy to see that an equivalent amount of fruit and vegetables needs to be added – say some tomatoes and green beans and half an apple. It is obviously also most useful if you can get your child to understand this way of looking at meals.

Do you need to get the balance right daily, or weekly, or over the course of a year? You might, for instance, get anxious if your child eats chips all day long on an outing. But this is unlikely to make a difference, assuming it is one exceptional day. Meals on other days will make up the 'balance'. But if it is chips all week, then this is another matter entirely and the balance will obviously not be achieved. It is probably best for parents to aim for certain intakes on a daily basis for their children, but if this is not achieved do not worry about it, as long as over a week you can see that the balance and variety issues are addressed. The point is that it is not worth worrying or rowing about one meal, but it is worth getting the balance right over a longer time.

Basic, Simple Guidelines

It is easy to get bound up with the details. Is my child getting enough iron? What is a portion of fruit and vegetables? How much milk is needed? You will find the answers to these, and other nutritional questions, in this book. However, if you follow the basic principles set out below, the details usually resolve themselves.

- Choose at least five portions fruit and vegetables daily – the easiest way to do this is to make sure at least one portion is served at each of the three main daily meals with two further portions as snacks (some carrot sticks and a piece of fruit, for instance).
- Breakfast should always be eaten no matter how rushed. Base the meal on the principles of the Balance of Good Health plate described above, as you would any other meal.
- Encourage your kids to enjoy their food and make it colourful. By enjoying a variety of natural colour in foods you automatically ensure a good nutritional spread, as well as making it visually appealing. For example, red fruit and vegetables are high in carotenes, green vegetables are high in magnesium and folic acid, and purple fruits are high in a potent antioxidant called proanthocyanidin.
- Make snack choices nutritious. By making wise choices you never lose the opportunity to pack in more nutrients. By making poor choices you lose that opportunity (*see* Munchies, page 169).
- Offer desserts by all means, but avoid using them as a bribe to eat up. Children then get mixed messages about 'good' food being something to be got through and 'bad' food being a reward. There are many healthy dessert options, *see* page 45 for ideas.
- Prepare mostly whole foods which are packed with nutrients. 'Functional foods' are the newest trend in foods, yet yoghurt, wholemeal bread, bananas, porridge, oily fish and other foods are the original functional foods, packed with the vital antioxidants, minerals, essential fats, fibre and pre- and probiotics that encourage good health.
- Favour cooking methods that preserve the intrinsic goodness and flavour of food and does not rely on a lot of added fats. Steaming, baking and gentle grilling are all good options.
- Drinks are important to remember to include in the balance. Very sugary drinks will tip the balance away from good health while water, diluted fresh juices, milk or milk substitutes will provide necessary nutrients.

School Meals and a Balanced Diet

School meals, or meals with a child minder, are likely to make up around a sixth of all the meals your child eats. This means that what your child chooses at these times makes an important contribution to overall nutritional balance. However, it also means that what happens at home is – relatively speaking – more important. While schools are required to provide nutritionally balanced meals (*see* School Catering, page 218), remember the proverb: You can lead a horse to water but you can't make it drink. Even though fresh fruit and vegetables are on offer at school, your child may not choose them. If you 'indoctrinate' your child (an unfashionable concept, but indoctrination is what it is) to enjoy fresh foods at home, and to develop a broad range of tastes, the chances of them making healthy choices at school are increased. At the very least, he or she is less likely to turn up their nose at what is on offer.

Best Behaviour and Concentration

Children's behaviour is the subject of much controversy, investigation and discussion. Are our children getting more out of control? What is good behaviour, and what is bad? Are 'moods' normal and natural? When are they out of control? Most children go through changes in behaviour patterns, depending on their age, their emotions and their exposure to outside influences, and parents can find it a challenge to keep up with these changes. Typically, children will experiment with different behaviour patterns to see what works and what doesn't – for them! They are constantly testing their boundaries and the boundaries set for them. By being prepared to talk about it, remaining firm about core values and always loving a child, most behaviour issues can be worked through. Children often do not have the verbal skills needed to address issues that are affecting them and patience may be needed. Just listening – really listening – to their viewpoint or concerns can be more than half the battle. But remember that listening does not mean jumping in with your own views all the time!

It is worth investigating the effects of nutrition on your child's behaviour. Important nutrients are needed for brain health, all of which impact on behaviour, balance of moods, depression and anxiety. Good nutrition is a major player for all of these and I would urge you to read Brain Food, page 24.

Nutritional Considerations

Some of the nutritional factors which affect behaviour, mood, concentration and attention span include:

Blood Sugar A wired child is an unhappy child and excess sugar or refined carbohydrates in the diet can be a contributing factor. Blood sugar levels which are on a roller coaster are not going to make focussing and paying attention any easier for a child (think how hard you find it to concentrate mid-afternoon after a large lunch or sugary snack). Keep sugary foods and drinks to a minimum, and instead concentrate on providing meals based on proteins, vegetables and complex carbohydrates. Stock up on snacks that do not make blood sugar swings worse (*see* Munchies, page 169).

Caffeine Parents who would not dream of giving their child a cup of coffee nevertheless fail to consider the impact of caffeinated fizzy drinks or lots of chocolate on their child's behaviour.

Food Additives Some children react badly to these and research has shown that even children who are not obviously allergic or sensitive can benefit from having food colourings removed from their diet. For more on this *see* Labels II – Additives, page 134.

Fatty Acids Just because these come towards the end of the list does not mean that they are the least important. As a priority, I would give any child with serious behaviour or attention span problems one or two daily supplements of fish oils (LCP) fatty acids supplements. For more on this, *see* Brain Food, page 24, and Learning Difficulties, page 142.

Hydration It is so easy to forget about water. I am not going to say too much here, as the subject is covered in detail on page 270, however do remember that just fractional dehydration will affect a child's ability to concentrate. Six to eight glasses daily is recommended.

Protein You don't need to worry about protein intake in the average child's diet. You may, however, want to think about a particular protein building block, or amino acid, called tryptophan, which is found in wheatgerm, pork, chicken, turkey, fish, other meats, cheese, cottage cheese, soya beans, cauliflower and broccoli. This is a large molecule that competes for transport with other amino acids and often loses out because of its size. Because tryptophan is used to make the brain chemical serotonin this is important. Low serotonin levels are linked to erratic moods, depression, poor sleep patterns and appetite control. In order to improve the transport of tryptophan into the brain it helps to include carbohydrates in a meal. This triggers insulin, which clears other amino acids out of the way, and gives tryptophan the opportunity to cross the 'blood-brain' barrier. In terms of children's health, this could be particularly important at night-time when you want them to get a good night's sleep and, indeed, carbohydrate and protein meals, such as a warm oatmeal and milk drink, are known to be soporific.

Success with Behaviour Problems in Schools

Recently, a few schools have received a lot of publicity because they have had tremendous success in improving behaviour patterns in their pupils by simply banning fizzy drinks, sweets, crisps and junk food, and introducing balanced meals, nutritious snacks and improved water intake. One headmaster said, rather tellingly, that when he first introduced these measures it was the parents, and not the children, who felt threatened and upset. In the meantime he saw, as have other schools:

- Improvements in concentration.
- Better, calmer behaviour.
- Improvements in attendance, both from reduced ill-health and reduced absenteeism.
- Reductions in staff turnover resulting from conflicts with children.
- Significantly improved exam results.

As he explained, these were not figments of his imagination, but quantifiable and measurable improvements, verified by attendance records, teacher 'incidence' reports and exam results. The turnaround happened in less than a year.

For more on what you can do to encourage positive changes in your child's school, *see* Parent Power page 191.

Other Important Considerations

Anxiety is commonly acknowledged as a childhood problem, especially when changes such as divorce, the arrival of siblings or moving house come into play, yet many parents are surprised to learn that children can also suffer depression. Obviously, with either depression or behavioural problems, one of the important places to seek answers is in behavioural counselling – not just for your child, but for the whole family. A child is, by-and-large, a product of the family environment. Speak to your doctor about where to find help.

Children are expected to sit still and concentrate for a relatively long time in many situations. If they find this difficult to do it is not uncommon for them to be labelled as having behavourial problems. Yet there is a great difference between a boisterous child and one who is hyperactive.

If a child has trouble paying attention another important thing to rule out is poor hearing. A hearing test at your doctor will provide answers. For more on this, *see* Food as Medicine: Ear Infections page 76.

Children need a regular sleep routine. One study found that irregular sleep patterns was linked to ADD (attention deficit disorder) symptoms, and medication was stopped or reduced just by improving bedtime routines. Certainly any child that is expected to concentrate during the day needs to have a decent night's sleep beforehand.

If a child is twitchy it could also mean that he or she is not getting enough time and space to burn off energy and steam. Time spent playing out of doors, rough and tumbling, is time well spent.

See also Learning Difficulties, page 142, and Energy, page 59.

Boost the Nutrient Value of Meals

In the real world (in which we live!) kids are not going to choose their foods to be perfectly balanced nutritionally. So it helps to have a few ideas up your sleeve to make sure that the content of their meals can be enhanced.

- Add extra vegetables or fruits to recipes at every opportunity or serve as side dishes.

- When you offer a sweet or chocolate for a snack your child is missing out on the opportunity to eat something that has real nutritional value, such as a yoghurt, a small sandwich or some fruit. One way round this is to automatically include these as part of a snack. So offer a cube or two of chocolate alongside a few slices of fruit, or a few crisps with a small sandwich square. This way you avoid the issue of 'deprivation' yet at the same time ensure that there is some balance to the snack.

- A child who is hungry may be more amenable to eating something healthy, so this may be the best time to offer some vegetable soup to start a meal, or some cruditées or salad to munch on while he or she is waiting for the rest of the meal.

- You can also take the surreptitious route by sneaking vegetables into a dish. If your child does not like chopped onions, you may find that puréeing them once they are cooked, so they disappear into a sauce as a flavouring, is acceptable. Likewise, vegetables on a plate might be passed over, whereas a tasty and warming vegetable or lentil soup is enjoyed or a vegetable based sauce on a pasta is fine.

- As your child becomes more independent and eats away from home instil one thing into him: to choose just one portion of fruit or a vegetable with each meal. This is the minimum to ensure good health and by keeping the message simple you have a greater chance of it being adhered to.

- Learn to adapt recipes to improve their nutritional content. Many recipes will tolerate having half the flour substituted with wholemeal flour or other grains such as ground oats or buckwheat – it is just a question of experimentation. You can also usually get away with reducing the amount of sugar in a baking recipe by one-third without affecting the quality. Another tactic is to replace some sugar with chopped or puréed dried fruit such as dates or raisins, which give good levels of fibre, minerals and antioxidants. You can also add chopped or ground seeds to both savoury and sweet dishes to add a nutty

flavour and boost the essential fatty acid, mineral and fibre
levels.

Brain Food

The human brain is pretty amazing, but most fascinating of all is a
child's brain. In the first few years the brain cells are linking up and
making billions of connections. At this young age children are like
sponges, absorbing information at a rate that is truly fantastic. In
fact, a three-year-old has a brain that is twice as active as an adult's.
This activity creates a huge metabolic demand on resources. In an
adult, a fifth of energy is diverted to the brain. Because children's
brains are relatively much larger than an adult's (as a ratio of body
size) this increases the demands made on energy levels considerably.
This is one reason that the calories a child needs, again compared
to adult/body ratio, is high.

There are several aspects of diet that impact on the nervous system,
and thus on our ability to concentrate, learn, balance behaviour and
have the energy to enjoy life. By choosing a varied diet, that includes
the foods and nutrients mentioned below, you will be doing your best
to help your child optimise his abilities. If your child has particular
learning or behavioural difficulties, you may want to apply this information with a little more determination.

Fatty Acids Fish has a well deserved reputation as a brain food and
science is firmly backing up the old wives' adage to eat more of it.
The fatty acids contained in oily fish, DHA (docosahexaenoic acid)
and AA (arachidonic acid), are essential components of the brain,
eyes and nervous system. DHA, which makes up to a third of the
dry weight of the brain, is as important to it as calcium is to the
bones. These fatty acids are important throughout life, but have a

particular benefit during a child's first few years, when the brain is still linking-up neurons (a process called arborisation). DHA is also needed to help build the fatty layer around the nerves, known as the myelin sheath, which speeds up nerve transmissions. The only time we manufacture DHA and AA in our bodies, however, is when mothers produce breast milk, which underscores its essential status for the infant's brain. Children of earlier centuries would then have had much more DHA than our children get today because more were breastfed and diets also favoured higher DHA levels.

Ideally, you should introduce oily fish at an early stage so that your children get used to eating it. Only 16 per cent of children in the UK eat oily fish (and a lot of that is probably canned tuna, which is low in these vital fats). One eminent scientist has stated that he thinks that this deficiency in children's diets is linked to poor mental development and behavioural problems in our society. If your child will not eat fish, and has learning problems, it is well worth getting him to take a fish oil supplement as an alternative. Another option for fish-shy children are the 'functional' foods which are now finding their way onto the market. Eggs, bread and yoghurts that are enriched with DHA (they have a symbol on the package saying as much) are now readily available.

Iron This is the most commonly deficient mineral in children, with 84 per cent of under-fours affected, and 57 per cent of over-fours. Iron is needed for building red blood cells and reduced levels impacts on cognitive skills. Iron deficiency is frequently caused by children being introduced to cow's milk too early, instead of being given fortified infant formula. Other causes include exclusively breast feeding for more than six months (it is important to introduce foods at this stage as, after this time children need more iron than breast milk alone can provide), vegetarian diets lacking iron, and also junk food diets.

Zinc This mineral is essential for all growth processes, including those of the brain. The diets of 72 per cent of children under the age of four are low in this mineral and it is important to include good sources on a regular basis. These are similar to those for iron, and include meat, fish, eggs, cheese, nuts and seeds. In adults, low zinc-status is linked to mental ill-health, including depression, nervousness and anorexia. If your child is listless or depressed you may want to ensure a good dietary intake.

Selenium This mineral, which is needed in only the tiniest amounts, is linked to balance moods. The best food sources are Brazil nuts, as well as wholegrains, fish, shellfish, meat, rice and seaweed.

B-Vitamins These are the ultimate 'nerve nutrients'. The whole group (B_1, B_2, B_3, B_5, B_6, B_{12}, folic acid), one way or another, are involved in nerve and brain health and energy production. Two of the richest sources are wheatgerm and brewer's yeast, which is one reason why long-suffering children of old were given spoonfuls of these, along with cod-liver oil. The science of nutrition is finally confirming what parents of earlier generations instinctively knew. Other good sources of B-vitamins are wholegrains, fortified cereals, milk, Marmite, liver, mushrooms, bananas, peas and green leafy vegetables. One of the anciliary B-vitamins is choline, from which the brain chemical acetyl-choline is made. Low levels of acetylcholine are linked to memory loss, which may be particularly important for children at exam times. Good food sources of choline are eggs, liver, soya, lentils and peanuts.

Iodine Deficiency of this mineral in the womb can lead to severe mental retardation in the baby, and in children and adults severe iodine deficiency leads to goitre and affects mental health. Iodine is the core molecule in the thyroid hormone, which regulates meta-bolism, and low thyroid hormone brought on by low iodine affects mental health. In the West this, thankfully, is largely a problem of the past, though we are now seeing a resurgence of borderline iodine deficiency in some children. Any adult who is diagnosed with low thyroid hormone function will know that the symptoms include low energy, poor concentration and 'fuzzy thinking'. Iodine-rich foods include all milk, dairy produce, eggs, meat, seafood and seaweeds, as well as sea salt and iodised salt. (Most of intake is due to adding iodine into animal feeds and using iodine compounds to sterilise milking equipment.)

Lead It is unfortunate to have to end on a bad note. One in ten children in the UK have blood lead levels sufficiently high to impair IQ. And this is according to government statistics. Lead is a nerve-toxin and it is still prevalent in our environment, even though the situation has improved since leaded petrol was banned. The most common sources of lead contamination are:

- Lead brought into the house in soil on shoes and then trapped in carpets and circulated in the air breathed indoors. Hard flooring and leaving shoes by the front door helps.
- Children licking fingers contaminated with house dust and soil.
- Old lead water pipes still act as conduits into many homes – you need to check yours if you live in an older house.
- Paint chewed off old lead-based paintwork and toys by younger children – this is much more common than you might believe, and if you have flaked paint on a banister in an old house you should attend to it. Beware, also, of sanding old paintwork, as this releases microscopically small particles that can be breathed in.
- Buying produce sold by the roadside.
- For more information check out www.leadsafehome.org.uk

Breakfast

Children certainly need to 'breakfast like a king' (or a queen). This essential meal is needed to replete blood sugar levels after the overnight fast, to provide fuel for the morning. Children who skip breakfast, or who consistently eat cereals high in sugar, do not perform as well in aptitude tests, both verbal and non-verbal, when compared to children who eat slow-releasing complex carbohydrates and protein.

Unfortunately, breakfast is also the time when parents are often at their busiest – packing children off to school and themselves off to work – and the nourishing breakfast has got lost somewhere in the hurly-burly. The quick breakfast has been highjacked by cloyingly sweet cereals and cereal bars, all targeted specifically at children. They can contain as much as 50 per cent sugar. Many cereals and cereal bars have a worse nutrition profile than chocolate bars and sweets and you wouldn't give your kids these for breakfast, would you? Even some brands of supposedly 'healthy' cereals such as muesli are highly sugared, quite simply because sugar is a cheaper ingredient than dried fruit and nuts.

Look on the side of the packet. Total sugars will be expressed in grams per 100 grams. So if it says 35 grams per 100g this means the product is 35 per cent sugar. And often it is a lot higher. Government guidelines say that more than 10 per cent in a product is too much. Ingredients are listed in order of weight, and any word ending in -ose or -ol, or which is described as malt or honey, is sugar. It is not unusual to see four different sources of sugar listed on a cereal packet.

So what are the healthy breakfast choices? Always include a piece of fruit, or a vegetable such as mushrooms or tomatoes. Always provide a drink, and aim, also, to give some complex carbohydrates and some protein. By ensuring that protein is included, it makes for more morning brain-power than carbs alone.

10 Breakfast Ideas

Five Time-to-Spare Breakfasts

- A bowl of old-fashioned porridge made with milk or soya milk. Sweeten with mashed banana and raisins.
- Boiled egg with wholemeal bread soldiers. Orange segments.
- Grilled bacon sandwich (using unsmoked, lean bacon with fat trimmed) with sliced tomato. Preferably using wholemeal bread.
- Grilled tomato and mushrooms with melted mozzarella on toast.
- Bowl of muesli with grated apple and sunflower seeds moistened with milk or calcium-enriched soya milk.

Five In-a-Rush Breakfasts

- Toasted cinnamon and raisin bagel with cream cheese. Glass of diluted orange juice.
- Some oatcakes spread with nut butter and jam. An apple.
- Low-sugar instant cereals such as Ready-Brek, corn-flakes or Weetabix. Serve with milk, or calcium-enriched soya milk or rice milk, chopped nuts and chopped dried apricots.
- Yoghurt with sliced fruit and toast with hummus.
- A slice of ham or cheese, wrapped in a slice of bread or added to a rye cracker with a chunk of cucumber. Glass of diluted mango juice.

Busy Parents

Juggling work with parenting is a huge issue for some people. Many people also find it awkward balancing the needs of working with finding the time to cook from scratch. When working on improving the family's healthy eating one of the hurdles that many parents need to overcome is the reality of frantically busy lives. It can seem like there is just not enough time in the day to chop, peel and prepare food, and mental fatigue sets in at the just the thought of what to make for the next meal. No wonder so many people fall back on the option of ready-prepared meals. This is not helped by the fact that there is, frankly, a whole generation of parents who have not learned basic food preparation and cooking skills and so the inertia linked to learning how to create from scratch can be hard to overcome.

But if you are determined to make strides in this department (and it is worth it!) there are many ways to change your family's habits. In the long run you make your life easier and healthier. The most time-effective way to deal with family catering is to make one meal for everyone – who has the time to cook two separate meals anyway? The only way you can do separate meals is if the quality of the food gives, and usually that means that the children are given convenience foods. Take the time to make these changes, and never lose sight of the importance of putting healthy eating higher up the priority ladder. It may seem like a lot to do initially, but it does get easier, and eventually it simply becomes a habit. Some tips:

- Take a few minutes each week to plan your shopping and menu ideas. Buying more fresh food will force you to cook more often. Earlier in the week prepare whichever foods are the least long-lasting. If you have spinach and cauliflower in the fridge, the spinach is best cooked immediately because the cauliflower will last three or four days perfectly well.

- If you are going to eat some pre-packaged, convenience, or take-away foods learn which are the most healthy, or at any rate the least unhealthy. *See* Convenience Foods – Healthier Options, page 37.

- Also, if you are going to eat convenience foods, learn to quickly and easily improve the nutritional content of the meal. There is nothing intrinsically wrong with a good quality pizza but if you add a mixed vegetable salad alongside it and finish with a piece of fruit then the balance of the meal will be that much better. *See* Boost the Nutrient Value of Meals, page 22.

- If your cooking skills need improving you don't need to throw yourself in at the deep end. Make a point of experimenting with just one new recipe a week. In no time at all, your repertoire will be much wider.

- When you do cook, make extra helpings. Taking time to prepare meals at weekends which can be frozen is one practical solution. You can freeze some to make an instant meal another day when time pressured. Or cook something one day that can serve as the basis of the next day's meal. Baked salmon is delicious cold the next day, extra rice could be used for a stir-fry, left over vegetables can be turned into a tasty soup, shredded chicken served with peanut bang-bang sauce and shredded lettuce in Chinese wraps (buy these fresh or frozen).

- Include your child in these experiments. By making food preparation a part of his life you will enhance the fun of cooking – it isn't always drudgery. By making cooking an 'activity' you do two things at once – you teach your children about good food, but you also engage and spend time with them.

Quick Main Meals

Concentrate on quick to prepare recipes. In virtually the same time it takes to heat a ready meal in the microwave you could:

- Stir-fry some vegetables and prawns and toss in cooked rice.
- Make a three-bean salad using canned beans and vinaigrette and stuff it into a wholemeal pitta pocket.
- Grill some chicken with rosemary, lemon and olive oil and serve with steamed green beans and a tomato salad.
- Cook some pasta, such as freshly made torteloni or ravioli available from supermarkets and delicatessens, and serve with a freshly made tomato sauce and vegetable sticks.
- Steam some cous-cous. Fry some onions until translucent, add frozen peas, frozen spinach and chopped red pepper and cook until the pepper is tender. Add flaked smoked fish, toss together with the cous-cous, warm through and serve.
- Barbecue or grill fresh sardines and serve with salad and a hunk of bread to mop up the juices.
- Make an omelette bursting with cooked vegetables and flavoured with Parmesan.
- Make bangers and mash, but boost the nutritional quality by using at least 85 per cent meat sausages, and mash swede or parsnip with the potato and serve with peas and carrots (frozen is fine).
- Make some tiny falafel (from a packet mix) and serve with a yoghurt and cucumber dip and char-grilled pitta bread fingers.
- Make an instant meal from fridge and store cupboard standbys – cold cuts, seafood salad, anchovies, tuna, roll mop herrings, olives, mushrooms-à-la-Greque, artichoke hearts, pickles, sauerkraut, cold bean salad, carrot sticks, tabouli, sun-dried tomatoes.

See also Kitchen Shortcuts, page 126.

Childminders

As long as your child is at home with you, you are in control of most of the food he eats, but when you leave him with a carer or at a playgroup you may want to make sure that your child's dietary needs can be met. These days, most playgroups are aware of the dietary needs of different children, though you may still have to do some groundwork. Childminders are as varied as the children themselves and careful interview will help you to select one whose approach to feeding children mirrors your own.

- Do a basic recce first to check out the facilities.
- Don't be afraid to ask questions and visit the kitchen.
- At a childminder's house you might ask what their children normally eat before giving away too much about what your expectations are – and be realistic, if there is a huge gulf it may not be possible to bridge it. Ask about their attitude to healthy eating and, if you need to, about their ability to deal with special

dietary needs (for instance allergies, vegetarianism, religious or ethnic diets).

- If you prepare a lunchbox or tea-time treat ask them to discourage food swapping if this is a concern to you – particularly with regard to allergies.

- Provide written guidelines on your needs. For example, if your child is a vegetarian you may want to list foods to be avoided, such as those made with gelatine or cheese made with rennet. They may be unaware, for instance, that vegetarian means no fish, or white meat, or even that avoiding meat includes foods such as sausages. You may need to explain this to them. For more information and advice, *see* Vegetarians and Vegans, page 246.

- Provide a list of positive suggestions that are easy to prepare and are cost effective. This is also helpful if you are concerned that the food on offer is not as healthy as you would like it to be. Offering easy suggestions takes the onus off your child-minder to think up ideas themselves. It could be as simple as asking them to provide a piece of fruit and some non-sugary yoghurt to boost the nutritional value of an otherwise 'iffy' meal and asking them to provide water instead of cordial.

- Occasionally, a childminder, nanny or school canteen worker may not take your requests regarding avoiding certain foods seriously or pass correct information along to other care workers. By and large, this will not do any lasting damage unless your child has a severe allergy – if this is the case then you need to pre-empt any possibility of this happening. Stick to your guns about any potentially dangerous allergies. There have been cases of childminders who have simply not understood the impor-tance of avoiding a particular food who have subsequently put a child at risk by feeding the child the food in question. All-too-frequent situations arise such as the following tragic case. A mother dropped off her infant child at a nursery. They had been instructed in the past that the child was severely milk-allergic and to keep dairy produce away from her food in the kitchen. The main carer handed over responsibility to a newer recruit who was also made aware of the allergy. She decided to feed the child some breakfast cereal, leaving out the milk. But she did not read the label on the cereal packet and was unaware that dried milk powder was one of the ingredients. The child developed serious respiratory problems and, despite her mother being called and getting to the nursery within minutes, died of an anaphylactic reaction. If you have an allergic child who is too small to be involved in their own food selection you must take all necessary precautions and take nothing for granted. *See* Peanut and Other Allergies, page 195, for more resource material which may be suitable for childminders, nurseries and schools.

Choice

We live in a society which values freedom of choice, and this extends to food choices. We also live at a time of unprecedented food availability in the West. In theory, this is a good thing – you can have all sorts of produce at all times of the year and people on tight budgets can select from a more varied diet if they know how to prepare inexpensive produce. The Government also takes a (by and large) pro-choice view and legislates very infrequently on matters relating to healthy eating, sticking mainly to food safety issues. Their approach is one of education to increase awareness of what the choices are. Again, in theory, this abundance of choice should be a good thing. But is it? And is it a good thing in relation to children's health?

The truth is that, with a couple of exceptions, healthy eating messages are struggling to get through to the people, and therefore the children, who need the information. Those in higher socio-economic groups have become more aware of healthy eating messages, but those in lower socio-economic groupings are seeing a deterioration in important health markers and the healthy eating messages are not really getting through efficiently to those who most need them.

The last time that a nanny-state approach to eating was enforced was during the Second World War. At that time there was rationing, people were urged to 'dig for victory' (in other words to grow their own food if possible), and specific targets and guidelines were put in place. The 'national loaf' retained fibre and nutrients which these days are taken out, and rationing meant that sugar consumption plummeted. At the same time, and as a result of this, children then enjoyed more vigorous health than their counterparts today, and the number of children suffering from dental decay resulting from sugar consumption also dropped dramatically.

Perhaps there is a case for reducing choice for children in what they eat? In cultures that value the importance of eating as a family, children do not have 'children's food' prepared specially for them. They have the same 'choice' that the rest of the family has – in other words they eat what everyone else does. This concept may seem at odds with educating your child about food and eating (see Learning About Food, page 138) but in reality it isn't, because reducing choice does not mean reducing variety in reality – in fact, it will probably increase it. For instance, if you ask the question 'What would you like to eat?' you should not be too surprised if the answer that comes winging back is 'A burger and a packet of crisps'. But if you simply say, 'We are having fish pie for supper tonight', then fish pie is what is going to be eaten.

Learning to appreciate food, food preparation and good health might need a more focussed approach. Remember you are working against the perpetual messages churned out by food advertising and by peer pressure. I do not propose to come to any conclusion in this section, but instead to leave it to you to figure out where you stand on this issue!

Convenience Food – Healthier Options

Our children have become convenience food addicts – and the only way this happens, face it, is if we buy these foods and stuff our larders full of them.

If you are serving foods such as sausages, nuggets or burgers, limit them to twice a week, and remember that the chances are that they will be getting them, anyway, at school once or twice weekly. When you do use these products, make sure you boost the general nutritional quality of the meal by adding vegetables and fruit, or plainly cooked starches such as potatoes or rice.

Convenience Comes at a Price

- We spend £600 million annually on ready-made pizzas.
- £360 million is spent on chicken nuggets annually.
- Sausages account for £200 million of our yearly shopping bill.
- We spend £83 million on oven chips each year.

Together these total more than £1.2 billion. We spend another £1.9 billion on ready-made package meals. All of these types are high in salt and fat, and low in nutrients.

You can also improve the situation by being selective about what you buy and making intelligent substitutions. Once you have done a bit of groundwork and identified products that fit the bill then the process becomes much easier. In no time, you will automatically reach for the cereals that have a better nutritional profile than the sugar-laden ones most often promoted to children. You will easily identify the sausages that contain 85 per cent or more meat, and leave the majority, which are around 65 per cent meat, and there-fore packed with one-third fillers and fat, on the shelf. The differ-ence in the pool of grease that results from cooking the two types of sausages tells you all you need to know. If you are going to give your child convenience or take-away foods these are the healthiest available:

Chips Choose those which are thick cut or those that can be oven baked without added fat. Even better, offer a baked potato.

Soups Tinned soups are high in salt and sugar. A much better option is one of the 'fresh' soups found in cartons in the chill cabinet. Serve with crusty wholemeal rolls instead of processed white bread.

Sausages Choose those which are 85 per cent meat. The mass-produced greasy sausage bears little resemblance to our proud heritage of really delicious, meaty bangers.

Beans Baked beans are about as healthy as convenience food gets, as long as you choose low-salt and low-sugar brands. Serve on whole-meal toast and you have a winner.

Fish Fingers These are not too bad as long as you choose the more expensive whole fillet brands. Compared to chicken nuggets, for example, they have about twice the 'meat' content and far fewer 'fillers'.

Fish and Chips As a treat once in a while, but not daily – pull off some of the batter and add in mushy peas or beans for a better nutri-tional profile. The supermarket versions, compared with those bought at the 'chippy', are much lower in overall fat.

Curry Now a more popular take-away than fish and chips! Choose plain rice instead of fried, and include a vegetable option such as chickpeas or peas and cheese in the menu.

Pasta Pasta is a healthy option as long as it is not laden with creamy sauces. Offering a tomato-based sauce is an ideal way to get another vegetable into the day. Toss in some broccoli florets while you are at it. Wholemeal pasta is an even better choice.

Pizza Avoid those with extra cheese hidden in the crusts, and stick to simple thin-crust pizzas. Ideally, encourage some vegetables amongst the toppings and eat with sliced tomatoes and cut up vegetable sticks.

Home Versions of Children's Favourites

It is by far the easiest plan for time pressured parents to develop a child's tastes towards eating the same food that the rest of the family eats. 'One meal for all, and all for one meal' – certainly when I was a kid children's choices were not generally available. However, we live in times in which the market for specific kid's foods has grown into a huge beast and it is hard to get away from that fact. This becomes particularly relevant when young friends come round for tea and all that the children will eat are sausages or nuggets. Fixing up batches of some children's favourites, when you have time to spare, and keeping them in the freezer for when you don't, can help.

Chicken Nuggets The average commercially available chicken nugget is a disaster area. It is less than 36 per cent meat, and is heavily laden with salt, low nutrient fillers and water. They also use the lowest quality meat from battery chickens that are routinely fed with anti-biotics as growth enhancers. To make your own, make breadcrumbs with 50 g of bread, put in a bowl and season. Beat two eggs in another small bowl. Cut three or four skinless chicken breast fillets into strips. Dunk the strips one by one into the egg and then into the bread-crumbs to coat on all sides. Heat some oil in a frying pan and fry them for about ten minutes until cooked through on all sides. You can 'par-cook' these more gently until cooked through but not overly browned and then freeze interleaved with greaseproof paper until needed. These can then be thoroughly defrosted and grilled until cooked through. You can also make fish fingers the same way, though these cannot be frozen. Serve with lemon.

Chips Chips with everything takes on a new meaning when you make them from scratch – 5 minutes of preparation, not much effort to cook, and the taste is a thousand times better than 'oven chips'. Choose baking potatoes for the right texture, scrub them clean (no need to peel), chop into chips, put a single layer in a baking pan with a fairly modest brushing of olive oil and bake in a medium-high oven until cooked (turn once or twice with a spatula and add a little bit more oil if needed, though the end result should be dry and not greasy).

Pizzas Buy ready-made bases or, even better, make your own dough in a bread machine. This is simplicity itself. It takes just a couple of minutes to check the recipe in the book that comes with the machine and to throw in the ingredients – you just need to plan a little ahead. Smooth over with salt-free tomato purée or passata, line up the toppings (such as ham, pitted olives, pineapple, mushrooms) for chil-dren to build their own, sprinkle on grated cheese, and bake in a hot oven for about 10–15 minutes.

Burgers Delicious burgers can easily be made with lean chicken breast meat and pear or with lean pork meat and apple. In a food processor chop 30 g of onion. Add 200 g of your chosen meat cut into chunks, and 50 g of fruit, and process on high speed until finely chopped but not mushy. Add some herbs if you wish. Form into patties. Fry, bake or grill in a tiny bit of olive oil on a medium heat, making sure to cook through. Serve on a bun with chopped salad, relish and sour cream. Extra, uncooked, patties can be frozen to defrost and cook another day.

Falafel This Middle-Eastern favourite, made from fava beans and chickpeas, is the ideal vegetarian alternative to burgers. Buy a ready-made dry mixture, add water according to the instructions, shape into small balls, and fry as directed. Serve inside warmed pitta pockets (wholemeal is best) with a chopped cucumber and tomato salad dressed with tahini and lemon dressing.

Sausage Rolls, Pasties and Samosas These are incredibly high in fat and usually include the worst imaginable quality of meat. Vegetable samosas are marginally better at around 20 per cent less fat. To make a delicious home version, keep ready-rolled filo pastry in the freezer for when you need it, or invest in a sandwich toaster (the kind that seals the edges). Put your filling in the middle of a square of pastry, fold into a pocket, seal and bake. Alternatively, fill in between two slices of bread and make triangle toasties. Fillings to mirror the convenience options could be high quality cooked sausages (add pickle for interest), cooked minced meat with onion and tomato (left over from when you are making a shepherd's pie), curried cooked chicken or curried cooked vegetables. Other fillings you could choose are as varied as your imagination – goat's cheese, sun-dried tomatoes and basil, ham, spring onion and grilled red pepper, or grilled aubergine with baked garlic and hummus.

See also Fast Food, page 68.

Desserts

From yoghurts to squeezy tubes and corners, mousses, jellies, custards and so on, they're convenient, kids love them, and while we know they're not nutritionally terrific are they all bad?

If they are having packaged desserts occasionally, with lots of fresh foods most of the time, then that is fine, but if (like the grown-ups on a bad night) they regularly get through a whole four-pack, then they could be heading for nutritional trouble. You also probably owe it to your children to taste these products before you serve them. The majority are cloyingly sweet and have a nasty stick-to-your-tongue quality to them. Ask yourself if these are the tastes you are happy to encourage in your children?

It really is worth putting some effort into giving your child the opportunity to enjoy real puddings – yes, they take a bit of time to organise, but I can't help but wonder at the marketing appeal of 'No fruit bits' and the texture of many pre-packaged desserts. While smooth textures might be fine for babies, my general feeling is that if we feed homogenous sweet pap to our children on a regular basis then we only have ourselves to blame if they turn away from real food with real textures as they grow up.

Yoghurts and Fromage Frais These can be some of the better choices, but often only because the others are uniformly awful. They are sources of protein and calcium, though at between 15–20 per cent sugar they give a hefty sugar kick. These days, most of them use acceptable colourings, though they are thickened with agents such as locust bean gum and guar gum, which shouldn't be necessary if the basic yoghurt was of a good quality in the first place. If you look hard enough, you can find decent yoghurts. But many come with assorted 'corners' where further inroads are made on the health qualities of the basic yoghurt by increasing the overall sugar levels. Fromage frais are denser but have more or less the same nutritional value as yoghurts. They are generally sold in much smaller pots and tubes and the expensive pricing reflects the extra packaging for a smaller amount of product. As *The Food Magazine* pointed out about one product, 'How to turn a milk drink into something with much higher profit margins: pack it into a tiny 50 ml sachets, and thicken up the milk with sugar. Not just a little sugar, but a total of 56 per cent of the product.'

Mousses They are either ready-made or come in packets to reconstitute. A mousse is meant to be light and fluffy, so this is just an excuse to give less product in the same size pot as yoghurts – water and air are simply whipped in to create products that weigh 60–70 g against 100–125 g for yoghurt. The other types of mousses are the ones you reconstitute from powder. The ingredients of a banana-flavoured package are pretty typical of most of them: (in order of quantity) maltodextrine, hydrogenated vegetable oil, modified starch, whey powder, emulsifiers, gelling agents, milk protein, flavourings, sweetners, colour. Not a banana in sight. And to cap it all, they blaze across the front of the packet 'No Added Sugar'. The reason they do this is that the product contains artificial sweeteners. Personally, I'd rather mash a banana with some plain yoghurt.

Jellies If the mousses are bad, pre-made jellies are awful. Jelly is mostly sugar and water anyway, so you can't ever hope that it is going to be a good thing, but these products are pretty horrible (*see* Labels II – Additives, page 134, for information on the colourings they contain). You can easily make your own with juice and vegegel (available from health food shops).

The Best of the Convenience Desserts

- Creamed Rice Pudding. Some top brands are just full-cream milk, skimmed milk, whey (milk product), rice and 9 per cent sugar. They also taste reasonable.
- The better children's cartoon yoghurts are 8 per cent sugar and with no artificial ingredients. Some of the better organic fruit yoghurts have no suspicious ingredients and the label mentions the healthy bacteria L. Acidophilus. Or organic fromage frais is another option.
- Children's soya yoghurt, suitable for those avoiding dairy products and also for those who just want to ring the changes. Fortified with calcium to mirror milk yoghurts, but also a source of healthy fats and live bacteria. At 11.9 per cent sugar, a bit high but still better than many competitors.
- Real ice cream or custard made with milk or cream and not too much sugar can be used to dress up fruit slices for a pretty good pud.

Custards A basic custard recipe is milk, egg, some sugar and vanilla flavouring. Some pre-made custards have sugar and thickeners coming way before any milk, with eggs being a rare ingredient. Check the label.

Ice Creams If you are choosing real ice cream – that is a product made with milk – your child will at least get some calcium and protein. But look at most labels and they contain hardened vegetable fat, sweeteners, artificial flavourings and colourings whipped to a mousse with lots of air. Choose wisely. Lollies are just water, sugar and artificial colourings but can be easily made by freezing juice or smoothie mixtures in lolly moulds.

Ideas for Healthy, Yummy Desserts

- Thick-set yoghurt with home-made fruit purée or mashed soft fruit (banana, peach, strawberries, etc). Puréed apricots or other dried fruit make a strong and delicious flavoured topping (soak dried fruit in water for half an hour and blend in a machine, adding a tiny bit more of the soaking water if needed).
- Home-made egg custard with berries
- Keep stewed fruit on standby in the fridge and serve with custard, yoghurt or ice cream. Extra stewed fruit can be stored in the freezer. Apple is a classic, but plums, berries and rhubarb can also be used.
- Make a crunchy muesli topping with oats, chopped walnuts and dates to stir into yoghurts.
- Baked apples are terrific. Core an eating apple, score around the 'equator' to stop it bursting, fill the centre with raisins, dried apricots or other dried fruit and bake in a dish with a little orange or apple juice until soft. Serve with yoghurt or ice cream.
- Grate some dark chocolate on to home-made puddings or ice cream and serve with strawberries for a classic combo.

- Make jelly with real fruit juice set with vegegel (a vegetarian alternative to gelatine which you can find in health food shops). Use this jelly as a basis for a trifle.
- Bananas baked in their skin go all gooey and yummy.
- Whiz up some soft fruit with yoghurt in the blender for an instant 'fool'. Add some chopped crystallised ginger for a new flavour.
- When you bake muffins or fruit loaf, or buy shop bought for that matter, always put some away in the freezer for another time. Freezing slices makes it easy to take out only what is needed.
- Smoothies can be set with vegegel in the fridge to make a 'pudding' consistency. Avoid using banana, which goes brown, instead use berries for a fresh pink colour. Top with flaked coconut or grated dark chocolate.
- Halva is a very sweet Middle-Eastern treat, and a little goes a long way, but as it is made with sesame it is also nutritious. Used sparingly, it can add sweetness to other dishes.
- It takes 5 minutes to make a crumble topping. Put 50 g wholemeal flour, 50 g plain flour, 50 g porridge oats, 75 g butter and 50 g soft brown sugar in a food processor. Pulse until roughly chopped and blended. Use to top stewed fruit and bake for 20 minutes. Add chopped almonds or other nuts for the last 5 minutes for added taste and texture, but watch to make sure they don't burn.
- Poached pears (use vanilla or cinnamon for a flavour 'twist') topped with chocolate sauce (just melt some good quality chocolate and whisk in a little cream if you wish).
- Home-made rice pudding with sultanas or, for an extra rich taste, add some coconut milk.
- Make your own ice cream (with just fruit, cream and sugar) using an ice cream maker – it so easy and children love to help out.
- Make your own lollies by freezing fresh pressed juices or

smoothies in ice cream moulds. Watermelon, melon, mango, strawberry and banana all work well.

Diabetes

Diabetes is dramatically on the increase, and this is related both to the increase in obesity in adults and children and also to the increased intake of sugar and refined carbohydrates in the diet proportionate to other constituents of the diet. There are two types, type 1 and type 2. Diabetes involves an upset in the body's ability to regulate insulin and blood sugar levels. Insulin is produced in response to any carbohydrates eaten and keeps blood sugar levels from rising too high. Over the years, uncontrolled high blood sugar levels result in tissue breakdown that leads to damage to blood vessels and eye tissue.

Type 1

Type 1 is when the pancreas is unable to produce insulin, and usually starts in childhood. This type of diabetic needs to have insulin injections for the rest of their life. Symptoms that might suggest diabetes include excessive thirst accompanied by a frequent need to urinate. This happens because the body attempts to get rid of the build up of glucose in the urine and thirst results to replace fluids. Other symptoms are tiredness and weight loss. For more advice on the diagnosis and management of type 1 diabetes refer to your doctor. Type 1 was called child-onset diabetes to distinguish it from type 2, which was called adult-onset. However, now that type 2 is affecting younger people this differentiation is no longer appropriate.

Type 2

This used to be called adult-onset diabetes, but, as mentioned above, this is probably no longer appropriate. For the first time ever in the UK, children of European descent (Asians and some other ethnic groups are genetically more prone to diabetes) have recently been diagnosed with type 2 diabetes, an occurence which has been linked to childhood obesity and has already been seen in the US. Type 2 happens when the body cells become desensitised to the effects of insulin, leaving sugar in the blood (because it can't get into the cells for use/storage), forcing the pancreas to produce more and more insulin to bring these sugar levels down, until it becomes exhausted and starts to produce less. The end result is similar to that of type 1. When it is advanced, type 2 diabetes needs to be treated with insulin in the same way as type 1. In the early stages, however, it can usually be controlled through diet and exercise. Children at risk of type 2 diabetes need to make changes in their diet which help to manage their blood sugar levels. The main strategies to adopt include:

- Eat regular meals to avoid excessive highs and lows in blood sugar.
- Cut out sugary drinks. Replace with water, sugarless tea and non-sugary milky drinks.
- Replace sugary snacks and desserts with fresh fruit and lower-sugar puddings.
- Eat wholemeal carbohydrates instead of refined carbohydrates.
- Include some protein with each meal or snack.
- Use the fruit sugar fructose, which has a low glycaemic index and so can be consumed, sparingly, instead of sugar for the occasional treat. It does not have the same negative effects on bloating that sorbitol, often called diabetic sugar, has when used in larger amounts.

- Eat nuts. They make good snacks and reduce the risk of diabetes when they are used on a daily basis, though they should be substituted for other fat sources to avoid excessive calories.
- Enjoy regular daily exercise (those on insulin injections need to check their blood sugar levels).
- Normalise weight if overweight, by eating healthily. Switch to low-fat dairy products.

For more information on diabetes in children and teenagers look up Diabetes UK www.diabetes.org.uk

See also Obesity page 177.

Disordered Eating

Disordered eating is very common in our society. It takes two principle forms – chaotic eating and eating disorders.

Chaotic Eating This is, in part, what this whole book is about, and there is lots of information dispersed throughout the book in relevant sections – Family Mealtimes, page 65, Convenience Foods – Healthier Options, page 37, and Obesity, page 177, are just some to look at. Chaotic eating can be linked to overeating, undereating, loss of appetite, loss of interest in food, stress and emotional turmoil. The causes of these can be many and are probably largely to do with lifestyle and personality habits built up over time. It is linked also to aspects such as time factors (usually too little time), educational factors (simply not knowing about food and food preparation) and to advertising pressures. The way to re-establish order out of chaos is to instigate regular meal times, ideally eating as a family, to buy mainly fresh foods, to learn about food preparation and to care about the quality of the food you and your family eats day in, day out. Aim to ensure a child with disordered eating habits, or with early signs of eating disorders, at least takes a multi-vitamin and mineral each day.

Eating Disorders Anorexia and bulimia are a whole different story to chaotic eating. Anorexia means, and involves, starving, while bulimia involves bingeing followed by purging using vomiting, laxatives or starving. An anorexic will often develop into a bulimic. This is a specialised area of nutrition and I do not propose to delve too deeply as it involves so many psychological aspects. Food is used as a punishment, to make up for perceived failures and as a source of comfort. Eating disorders usually involve an altered body image. About one in ten girls aged 12 and up show signs of eating disorders, and girls as young as eight are being admitted for treatment. Girls involved in gymnastics and other high intensity sports have a much increased risk of eating disorders and may be attracted to these sports precisely because of their body image issues. Boys are much less frequently affected, but the numbers are on the increase.

Often parents are the last people to know when their child develops an eating disorder. This is because children with eating disorders are masters of disguise and are able to fool their parents for a very long time, by hiding food, wearing bulky clothing and other means. It is imperative if your child is not growing or putting on weight that you take appropriate measures to find out if an eating disorder, or other cause, is involved. Particular danger times are puberty, exam times and times of emotional upset (say a split in the family). Often parents do not want to know that their child is suffering from an eating disorder and this can delay discovery and diagnosis. A child should never be made to feel guilty, as they are already carrying a heavy burden. It is unlikely they are doing this deliberately, even if it started that way, and are often simply carried along on a wave they don't understand. Children with eating disorders are, however, extremely manipulative and can be confrontational, particularly with their parents, and it often takes people outside the immediate family to help the child to make the decision to seek help. It is important to listen to a child carefully, but rarely is a parent the right person to give that child advice. It is very important not to comment on appearance, body image and food intake. It is important to teach your child to feel good about herself, to not set ridiculously ambitious targets in various areas of life (such as homework, exercise and a perfectionist attitude to exams), to help them to adapt to their changing and developing bodies, and to be critically aware of the body images portrayed in the media. Emphasise the health properties of food rather than the calorie content or fat levels. Do not use food as a reward or punishment, and keep mealtimes as low-pressure, enjoyable times. You must seek professional help, and remember that children with eating disorders need a lot of love.

For help with eating disorders, contact the National Centre for Eating Disorders, 01372 469 493 or www.eating-disorders.org.uk

Other useful organisations include the Anorexia and Bulimia Nervosa Association, 020 8885 3936, or Overeaters Anonymous, 01426 984 674.

Drink to Health

There is much confusion about what constitutes a healthy drink for children. In truth, the only liquid that has a completely clean slate is water. Everything else has pros and cons. If you think about it, affluent Westernised societies are the only ones that bring children up on an array of sugary, and often caffeinated, drinks. Average soft drink consumption by children has risen from 13 g daily to 446 g daily – 15 glasses each week – a 34-fold increase since the 1950s. Soft drinks are now drunk by 90 per cent of children, so it is not surprising that half of them suffer from dental erosion. The issues surrounding the various types of drinks that your child might be attracted to are discussed below, and is followed with suggestions about how to make changes. For information on water, *see* page 270.

Sodas and Colas These really are a dietary minefield. I have never understood why parents think these are OK for a treat. Why 'treat' your child so badly? Many children drink them every day and a large minority drink them several times daily. There is nothing to recommend them at all and quite a lot of evidence that they are just plain detrimental. If they are caffeinated this is not wise for children, as caffeine is a strong stimulant that can interfere with sleep patterns, it is also a diuretic and it increases calcium excretion. If they are low-sugar then they will contain artificial sweeteners which are also a bad idea (*see* Sweeteners, page 228). And because they are still acidic they will also contribute to tooth erosion. But worst of all, and few people are aware of this, is the phosphoric acid contained in fizzy sodas which has a serious effect on calcium balance, causing a loss in the urine. At the age when children need to be building up bone mass, those who are regularly drinking sodas and colas are at risk of reducing it. *Recommendation*: Ban them.

Sports Drinks These drinks are pretty nifty in marketing terms. There is no evidence that children need them, even if they are very active. As with sodas and colas, they have a strong hit of sugar, and often contain caffeine and tooth-eroding acid. Of course they appeal to children. *Recommendation*: Water is best for sports performance (*see* Exercise and Sport, page 61, for an alternative sports formula). Ban them.

Cordials and 'Fruit' Drinks Cordials are often used by parents to make water more palatable. This can be based on their own tastes and dislike for 'straight' water. The main problem here is that children are not being trained to enjoy plain, clear, delicious water, which is what is really needed to quench a thirst! Parents will often chose a 'kind' version of buffered cordials which reduces the risk of tooth erosion when compared to other cordials, but these are full of sweeteners (*see* Sweeteners, page 228). Drinks for children must not, by law, contain artificial sweeteners but manufacturers get round this by saying that their drinks are not specifically aimed at children, which is nonsense. Many cordials also use colourings that may have adverse effects on some children (*see* Labels II – Additives, page 134). The companies that sell pre-mixed 'fruit' drinks employ marketing tricks to convince parents that their products are nutritionally equal to fruit juices. They carry pictures of fruit on the labels and flashes saying things like 'With Vitamin C' (which has been added in). But in reality they will contain as little as 5–15 per cent juice, the rest being water and sugar. In fact, half of juice drinks have more sugar than colas. They use vegetable oils, thickening agents and colours to make them look like fruit juice. They even have the nerve to package these drinks in bottles that look like fruit juice bottles and store them in fridges in shops – you could store them in the heat for a year and they would not go 'off'. *Recommendation*: Use cordials very sparingly, and not as a matter of course, and ban 'fruit' drinks.

Juices The best juice option, after freshly-made juices, are those that say 100 per cent juice on the carton (*see* box overleaf). *Recommendation*: One glass daily counts as one portion of fruit (but more than this does not count). They are good sources of vitamins and other nutrients (orange juice contains vitamin C, folic acid, potassium and flavonoids, for example). As they are still acidic, and so increase the hazard of tooth erosion, the recommendation is to limit consumption to meal times. As they also provide quite a sugar 'hit' from the fruit sugars they contain it is best to dilute them with water by half to two-thirds.

Tea Only 50 years ago this was the most popular drink to give children after water. Now that we give our kids colas and juices, tea is not so popular. Giving weak tea (cooled to a temperature that is tolerated) to children has some advantages as it is full of antioxidants for general health and also contains natural fluoride for healthy teeth.

The minute you add sugar it is not so great, but if sugar is demanded you can probably get away with half a teaspoon against two to four teaspoons in a cordial or juice. The only major disadvantage with weak tea, apart from a mild caffeine hit, is that tea quite dramatically reduces absorption of iron from plant foods, and so is probably best served away from meals (milk in tea reduces this effect). *Recommendation*: Enjoy in between meals.

Understanding Juice Labels

- Freshly Squeezed — What it says with no additives. Normally unpasteurised and kept in the chill cabinet, they have a shelf life of just a few days.
- Fruit Juice — 100 per cent juice, chilled or long life. Made by squeezing juice from the fruit or reconstituted from concentrate.
- Not From Concentrate — 100 per cent squeezed juice, no additives, pasteurised to extend chilled shelf life up to five weeks.
- From Concentrate — 100 per cent juice, reconstituted from concentrate, pasteurised. (Concentrate is used to reduce shipping and storage costs. Water is evaporated and then added back in later.)
- Hybrid — You won't find this term on the packs but some have a combination of Freshly Squeezed and Not From Concentrate or From Concentrate.
- Juice Drink — A minimum of 5 per cent juice with mainly water, sugars, sweeteners, flavouring and possibly additives.

Fruit Teas These are increasing in favour amongst parents looking
for a colourful alternative to cordials with a health 'twist'. The only
problem with fruit teas served on a regular basis is that they are acidic
and can contribute to tooth erosion. *Recommendation*: Serve with
meals only to reduce problems of dental health.

Delicious Drinks

There are times when just water doesn't appeal. Instead of resorting
to non-nutritious, tooth-eroding cordials, or worse, here are some
ideas for treats. But remember that drinking water is what our ances-
tors have done for millennia and water is still the healthiest drink of
all.

- Make a smoothie with fresh soft fruit in a blender. A banana,
  some strawberries or blueberries, melon, papaya, peaches –
  anything goes. Use water, orange or apple juice, milk, soya milk,
  rice milk, oat milk or yoghurt as the liquid element, depending
  on how thick you want it to be and what flavours your child
  enjoys. A handful of ice crushed at the last minute makes it
  refreshing in the summertime.
- Using 100 per cent carton juice or, even better, juice you have
  made, dilute with sparkling mineral water to make a fizzy drink
  that rivals any revolting soda for good taste. Decorate with a
  slice of lime, lemon or mint leaves.
- Old-fashioned lemonade uses lemon juice from either a half or
  a whole lemon – or lime for a change – mixed with straight or
  fizzy water, a teaspoonful or two of sugar (still less than in a
  soda) and some ice cubes for a 'clink' effect.
- Hot chocolate is a lovely treat and don't let the 'food police' put
  you off it! Use a very high quality chocolate powder, such as
  Green and Black's, or melt some good quality 60 per cent cocoa

solid chocolate. Use milk or calcium-enriched soya milk warmed up to drinking temperature to dilute to taste.

- Miso soup is a savoury clear drink, made from soya, which is available from health food shops. It has a beneficial effect on digestion. It is, however, just as salty as stock cubes or Bovril unless you use white miso or sweet miso which are less salty.

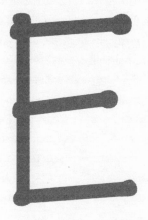

Electronic Nanny

The 'Electronic Nanny' has a lot to answer for! Yet let those of us who have not put our children in front of the telly to get some peace and quiet 'throw the first stone' . . . All but a few parents succumb, at least from time to time, but there are some important issues to consider.

Children who eat in front of the telly spend more *total* time in front of the box than children who don't, and studies have linked excessive TV-time to overweight problems in children. The most likely reason for this is that they are more sedentary than their non-TV-eating-and-watching peers. When the amount of time they spend sitting in front of the television is added to that spent sitting at their computers and playing electronic games it is not surprising that the amount of exercise they get can be minimal. Over time, the children studied increased their viewing time, and the number of TVs, VCRs and computers in children's bedrooms and eating time in front of the telly also increased. Each meal eaten in front of the TV added between half-an-hour to over an hour of overall watching time per day. That's a lot of sedentary time without social interaction. Yet another study has found that many parents and children now communicate with 'grunts' precisely because of TV-watching and this is affecting children's verbal skills.

As well as being sedentary, these children are also, inevitably, more exposed to advertising aimed at children. Some of that advertising is truly astounding. It is well worth making a point of sitting down with your children and watching some of the kid's advertising with them to understand what they are exposed to. For more on advertising aimed at children, *see* page 4.

Limiting the amount of TV watching is a first step. But avoiding a battle is probably desirable, so you will need to invest a little time in thinking of other activities – such as old-fashioned, round-the-kitchen table things involving paper and colouring pens, outdoor activities or helping you to concoct meals.

To wean kids away from the box to the family table you need to be firm and set an example. Building up a habit of family meal times could be the best investment you ever make. Make meal times pleasant and avoid rowing at all costs. Think of topics for conversation ahead of time, or invite friends to share meals – anything to distract from the TV and the chance of a row. Initially, avoid scheduling meals at times of favourite programmes, which is only asking for an argument, or video the programme and allow your child to watch it later. But keep eating away from the TV if you possibly can.

Other ways of combating the omnipresent monster (given that you are not going to get rid of it totally, though some people do), include not allowing a TV in your child's bedroom, planning with your child what they want to watch and only allowing those programmes, and avoiding having it on as background noise by turning it off when it is not being watched. In general you want to avoid the instant link of 'I'm bored, I'll watch TV'. There are lots of other things to do, and anyway it probably does not hurt kids to be a bit bored from time to time and to learn to have reflective time.

Energy

The utopian ideal for any parent is to have a calm child with nice even energy levels. The reality is that many children have peaks and troughs of energy throughout the day. This is perfectly normal in most cases, though both high and low energy levels can get out of control and be symptoms of something else that needs more investigation.

Sleep and Routine

Children respond best to a regular sleep pattern and routine. This is bound to be upset from time to time, say when travelling or at major celebration times. Rather perversely, when a child is tired instead of becoming listless they can become overwrought and wired. Children often do not know how to say they are tired and the parent needs to look for clues. One study established that cases of hyperactivity were resolved by the simple measure of establishing specific bedtimes and ensuring adequate sleep. Children need much more sleep than adults as their energy reserves are needed for growing. *See* Zzzzzzz . . ., page 279, for more.

Run It Off

Children with excess energy, or who are cantankerous, often just need to get out of doors and run off some steam. If your child is cooped up indoors for too long then he might just need to get out (even if he says he doesn't want to!).

Sugar Binge

The most common reason for both excessively high energy levels and low energy levels, is when children are on a sugar or caffeine roller coaster. For more on this, *see* Best Behaviour and Concentration, page 18, Drink to Health, page 51, and Munchies, page 169.

Food Colourings

If your child is having energy regulation problems he might be reacting to artificial food colourings. For more on this, *see* Labels II – Additives, page 134.

Anaemia

If your child is pale and listless and lacking energy over a period of time you need to take him along to your doctor to check for iron-deficiency anaemia. Children commonly do not get sufficient iron in their diet and this can exacerbate low iron stores that might have been a problem since birth. Increasing iron-rich foods in the diet is beneficial. The easiest way to do this is to serve liver once every two weeks, or red meat about three times a week, and to serve a small glass of orange juice with meals to maximise the absorption from plant sources of iron (the vitamin C doubles iron absorption). Do not attempt to treat anaemia yourself without a correct diagnosis. This is because, first of all, the listlessness may be a result of something else which needs checking out, and, secondly, because it is not appropriate to give a child iron supplements unless they need them. Gentle forms of iron supplementation, such as Spatone+(0800 7311 740 www.spatone.com), to be given after a correct diagnosis, are best. Herbal blood tonics which boost iron levels and are gentle for children are Floradix, nettle tea and beetroot. Another is Ferrogreen (08450 606070).

Exercise and Sport

The days of children with scraped knees from climbing trees, riding bikes round the neighbourhood or playing hopscotch in the road is now, regretfully, pretty much a thing of the past. With the advent of TVs, computer games and concerns about safety during unsupervised outdoor play, the opportunity for children to run about has been much reduced. Added to this the daily walk, or bike ride, to school that was almost compulsory for many children has all but disappeared. On top of this, schools have reduced the range of sports as they cut back on their budgets.

The British Heart Foundation has found that one in three children aged two to seven do not achieve the minimum recommended levels of exercise. At age 15, two-thirds of girls are inactive. Sport may be particularly important for girls, as impact exercise helps to build up bone density and protect against osteoporosis later in life. More boys than girls in the 15-year age group participate in sports.

Children need around an hour a day of running around and exercise. If your child is not getting this you should try to get him interested in a sport that he finds motivating. If your child does not do much exercise you may have to start slowly and build up. With improved nutrition energy levels should also improve. Once you have got the motivation element sorted out the rest should follow. You may have to set some strict rules to limit TV and computer game time and be prepared to go through a battle or two about this.

Setting an example is ideal and you can probably find something you want to do together, such as swimming, tennis or playing football. If your child is unwilling to go outside, try other tactics. Dancing and gymnastics are popular or a lower intensity activity such as yoga, which is great for flexibility, learning to breathe properly and 'centring' or calming a child down, might appeal to children who are non-competitive by nature.

If your child is physically very active it is even more important that he eat well and understand the basic concepts of good nutrition. You can use the analogy of putting high performance fuel into a Formula One racing car.

- Kids are easily influenced and large confectionary, cola and fast food companies not only sponsor football teams but also issue guidelines on 'healthy eating' for sports. Obviously the information they put out tends to have an angle. A typical example, while explaining the need to eat carbohydrates before during and after matches (see the next point), makes no distinction between the complex and simple (sugary) kind. This is very clever of them and completely insidious.

- Carbohydrate loading is used to maintain the energy available for longer endurance by keeping glycogen (the body's instant energy stores) topped up, but the quality of the carbohydrate is important and a banana or low-sugar cereal bar is a better option that chocolate, sweets or glucose. You only need to think about carbohydrate loading if the sport goes on at high intensity for over an hour.

- Sports drinks are unnecessary for most children. The exception to this is when sports go on at high intensity for about 90 minutes. Sports drinks help to rehydrate because of the electrolyte balance of sodium and potassium provided. They also provide sugar for glycogen stores. If you are going to use one, make sure it has 4–6 g of sugar per 100 ml and not more. A cheaper and perfectly effective option is to dilute one part fruit juice to two parts water and offer that, in a snazzy sports-drink container to make it a bit more 'cool'.

See also Obesity, page 177.

Faddy Eating

Food fads are the bane of many parents' lives and half of all children aged two to six go through this stage. But, take heart, food fads are not a fixed thing. You can find that your child refuses a food for months on end, and then just eats it again as if nothing has changed. It is best if you do not pass comment and just offer different foods until the fad passes. It could just be a test of your endurance.

The best way to avoid faddiness is to give your child a variety of foods, tastes and flavours from a young age, as often as possible. If you leave introducing, say, broccoli until they are five then you probably have to overcome some resistance. But if you give it to them from the start it will be enjoyed. What you have on offer also makes a difference. If the fruit bowl is always out then that is what everyone eats for dessert. But if your child knows there is a stash of chocolate biscuits then the chances are that they will head straight for those.

When persuading your child to try new foods make a deal that he can spit it out if he doesn't like it (provide a napkin to make this more discreet!) but he must at least give it a go. Don't assume that because he did not like something one time round that he won't like it at a later date, or in a different guise. Research has shown that children generally need to be offered a new food eight to ten times before they will find it acceptable. So if you give up after only three attempts, inadvertently, you aren't staying the course. Persistence pays!

As often as not, dislikes are 'acquired'. Because your child's best friend does not like onions nor does he. You can always use peer pressure in a positive manner and invite little friends round who eat well and enjoy a variety of foods.

Remember to serve small, manageable portions. Also serve food at a temperature that can be eaten. Children do not like to wait for food to cool down and their mouths are sensitive to temperature extremes. Waiting at table can give them time to think of reasons to not eat what is on offer.

It is also common for parents to prejudice their child's choices with their own likes and dislikes, which is a shame and is best avoided if possible. It might not even be a question of your own food choice but your beliefs about what children should and should not like. For instance, you might think that certain strong tasting foods are unlikely to be accepted and yet small children who have not been told otherwise often like strong flavours such as olives, anchovies, salami or curry.

Do not fall into the trap of offering biscuits or crisps just to get any food into your child. Let hunger take over and the fare on offer will probably be eaten at the next meal or the one after. Kids will often use meal times as an opportunity to assert themselves over their parents. They know how to pull your strings! If they get a reaction they are triumphant. While it is a good idea to educate your child about the relationship between food and health, it is a bad idea to always link it to times when the disputed food is in front of them on the table. By always saying 'eat it, it's good for you' the chances are that you will simply turn your child off. Better to leave the health stuff for more constructive times. Likewise, always offering a reward for eating up is linking the meal in the child's mind to a chore that needs to be got over. Nor should you threaten punishment for not eating up. Better to not remark on the lack of eating but simply to wait until the next meal. If in-between snacks are sought make them light – water and a piece of fruit or a single oatcake – and an appetite will be assured at the next meal.

One in five families fight at every meal, but this will just perpetuate negative feelings about food and eating together. It is really important when dealing with food fads to take the heat out of the situation. Getting upset about it does no good and is counter productive. Eat together as often as you are able (*see* Family Mealtimes, page 65) because children copy adults in their food choices and table behaviour, but for goodness sake make it a pleasant experience.

Avoid labels such as 'he's a picky eater' or 'she's a difficult child' or 'what a fusspot'. Not only is it not very polite, but this can perpetuate a child's view of how to behave. The carrot works much better than the stick, so offer lots of praise along the lines of 'well done, you've . . . cleared your plate', '. . . tried a new food', '. . . eaten five fruit and veg today'.

It is also a good idea if parents take the same line and agree with each other. One may take a softly-softly approach and be gently coaxing, while the other gets in a froth. Aim to hammer out a parental policy on this matter and then speak with the same voice.

Family Mealtimes

Your family eating habits will owe a great deal to your cultural background. In many cultures it is normal for families to eat together and children take this as the expected pattern. However in the UK and the US this habit has broken down to the extent that almost half of all families with children under the age of 12 rarely eat as a family.

The grazing, snacking, munching, TV dinner-eating, fast-food and take-away mentality has become the accepted norm.

This is a shame on so many levels. The social interaction of eating together is lost. Children may not even know what a 'square meal' looks like. Yet the home is the chief place of education about food. In a world bombarded by convenience, advertising and fast foods, which is even evident in schools, the home has the main responsibility for nutritional health and wellbeing. The trend in food education in schools has moved away from the basics of learning how to boil an egg – which, if you think about it, is pretty fundamental – and now centres on remote subjects such as 'food technology'. As parents, we really can't pass the buck. Children learn by observation, and they are more likely to eat a wide variety of foods if they see their parents doing so on a regular basis. Eating together helps to transfer belief systems and behaviour codes just by observation – not by enforcing a list of rules. Small actions such as passing food to one another teaches a child to share, and helping to set and clear the table teaches responsibility.

Aim to create a relaxed and pleasant atmosphere at mealtimes. Imagine you are a fly on the wall – what do your mealtimes sound like? Are they are stream of instructions such as, 'eat your veg', 'behave', 'don't eat with your fingers', 'chew properly', or are they a forum for the interchange of ideas and news?

Rules, such as you have them, need to be age appropriate. Two year olds may find it hard to sit still at a table, so let them wander off and make sure to welcome them back when they are ready. Five year olds, on the other hand, are more able to sit and participate in a meal and conversation, but remember to include your child as it is easy for grown-ups to talk over their heads about other things. If conversation regularly dries up, think about this ahead of time – there might, for example, be something in the newspaper that catches your eye which you can all talk about. Also change the seating arrangement from time to time and see what effect this has on conversation. You'll be surprised at the effect it can have. Remember, too, to have some fun: your child can pretend to be a waiter; collect flowers from the garden for the table; eat by candlelight; spread a paper tablecloth and provide colouring pens; eat with chopsticks.

If you are unable to sit down together for meals on a daily basis, make a point of doing so at least once or twice at weekends. During the week, at least sit down with your children and have a cup of tea while they are eating, as often as you are able, so that they are not relegated to eating on their own or just with other children. Incidentally, single-parent families are just as much a family as those with two parents, and while a single working parent may have more time pressures it is still a good idea to make the time to sit down together.

Ideas for Family Eating

While it is ideal if your child enjoys a wide variety of types of meals and cuisines, there is no doubt that there are times when some comforting family favourites are the only thing which will hit the spot. The following are a few suggestions:

- Vegetarian chilli, or chilli con carne, with rice
- Roast chicken with lemon and rosemary, vegetables and roasted baby potatoes
- Cheesy spinach pasta bake
- Wild mushroom and asparagus risotto
- Fish pie
- Pheasant casserole (with onions, carrots, parsnips, mushrooms)
- Mild prawn and vegetable curry with rice
- Chunky soups, such as pea and mint, or leek and potato, or fish soup
- Meatballs in tomato sauce with cous cous
- Stir-fry with vegetables, chicken strips or tofu and rice
- Liver, lentils and onions

Fast Food

There is plenty of evidence that our children are becoming junk food junkies. The main problems with this are:

- The menus typically on offer are excessively high in salt, saturated and hydrogenated fats and sugar. A child's burger meal with a pudding, for instance, will give four year olds double their daily intake of salt, two-thirds of their daily saturated fat intake, and two-thirds more than they need of sugar for the day. For seven to ten year olds it still takes them way over their daily needs.
- Fast food encourages a taste for monotonously similar foods which depend on salt for flavouring. There is no subtlety of taste developed which more varied food choices provide.

It is worth fighting the encroachment of fast-food restaurants. According to Sam Craig's immensely readable *Little Food Book*, one in every four Americans visits a fast-food restaurant each day. And we all know that where the US leads, food and healthwise, the UK usually follows.

Given that only the most dogmatic parents succeed in avoiding fast-food restaurants totally, the most likely success strategy is to limit the intake of fast-food meals to the odd occasion. Actually, if this is the norm in your family, a child will not even think about them most of the time. As often as not, with small children, it is not the food they actually want, but the little plastic collectable toys that are on offer – which just about says it all. The occasional fast-food takeaway is not really the issue, but if your child is eating at these places three or four times a week, as statistics confirm many children are, then you will want to do something about it.

Burgers

The burger restaurants have really got kids figured out. Little individual boxes, special kiddie-meals and collectable toys. It all adds up to a wise investment on their part as they snare their customers of the future. A few give-aways will ensure a lifetime of loyalty.

The big chains are very keen these days to issue leaflets that state that their beef patties are 100 per cent beef and that the cuts of chicken used are prime. However, you can't get away from the fact that a single child-meal contains twice the recommended amount of salt for a child's entire daily intake. Most of the products are also sources of unhealthy hydrogenated fats. The trick comes with simplicity and a flame grilled option is probably the best. A child-sized hamburger, or chicken nuggets, with chips contains around 37 per cent of calories from fat. While this is on the high side it is more respectable than the egg and sausage sandwiches on offer, where the fat content of the meal rises to 50 per cent of calories from fat.

Some burger chains are feeling the 'health pinch' and are offering salad bars and even fruit, and while this is an improvement they still need to address the health qualities of their basic meals.

Fish and Chips

This staple of the British high street is a favourite with kids. Looking on the bright side fish and chips (or chicken and chips) provides all the three macro-nutrients: proteins, carbohydrates and fat. Chips also provide useable amounts of vitamin C. But, realistically, this is one of the fattiest options with around 50–60 per cent of calories coming from fat. Nevertheless, because of all the growing they have to do, children can get away with these calories, so while you are struggling with your waistline, your children should, theoretically, be running it off. On the downside, fish and chip shops rarely offer child portions, which usually means that you end up polishing off the left-overs! Most chippies offer mushy peas and baked beans which will enhance the meal by increasing the fibre level and lowering the overall percentage of fat in the meal. The worst options on the menu are the pies, pasties, sausages in batter and deep-fried scampi, which are just fat masquerading as food.

Pizza and Pasta Restaurants

Pizzas are basically fairly nutritious – how bad can bread, tomato, some cheese and a few herbs be? It's the endless innovations that turn them into an artery-clogging option. A deep-pan pizza has 50 per cent more fat than a thin crust, and the latest new option, the stuffed crust, has twice the salt content of a thin crust. Luckily, small children tend to go for the simpler versions, such as the margherita, but older children often end up on the slippery slope, choosing salami and extra cheese, both of which are very high in saturated fats and salt. Encouraging your child to eat vegetables is an important health goal and pizzas are a great way to persuade your child to eat onions, peppers, mushrooms, spinach, peas, capers, olives and sweetcorn. Fishy toppings are also a great choice.

Avoid, if possible, the deep-fried choices such as potato skins, coated mushrooms and cheese-topped garlic bread as all change the focus of the meal towards more fat and salt. A trip to the salad bar is always going to be a good add-on, but problems lie in priming their tastes for the future with creamy dressings, so encouraging a taste for healthier olive oil-based vinaigrette is a wise investment.

Most of the pizza restaurants offer pasta as an option, and it is also on offer in a wide variety of family restaurants. This is usually a good choice. If your child prefers tomato-based sauces instead of creamy ones, so much the better, as you are sneaking another vegetable portion into the diet, but baked dishes with lots of gooey melted cheese on top are another way of increasing the saturated fat and salt level of the meal.

Drinks and Desserts

In most fast-food restaurants, the drinks are a minefield. Of the eight or so choices of soft drinks usually on offer only water, orange juice (not squash) and weak tea are choices that could be described as healthy options. There is nothing like water to quench a thirst, especially with a saltier-than-normal meal.

When it comes to desserts – funny how kids always have room for these – again simple is best. A scoop or two of ice cream is not a bad choice as it is rich in calcium (as long as it is really dairy ice cream). But again, some restaurants manage to mess this up by offering unlimited gooey sauces and toppings, loaded with artificial colourings, to say nothing of the sugar levels. Wouldn't it be nice if they offered some fresh fruit salad to go with the ice cream?

For some aversion therapy, read Eric Schlossers's *Fast Food Nation*. It will put you off fast food for life.

For wiser choices *see* Convenience Food, page 37.

Food as Medicine

The main function of food is nourishment and pleasure. However there are times when it pays to acknowledge the impact that food choices can also have on many of the diseases that affect us and our children. We've seen an inexorable rise in some childhood diseases – often labelled diseases of affluent societies – and there is no doubt that diet is a player in many of these. This is because the foods our children consume and the overall balance of their diet can either support or hinder the workings of the immune system, the digestive system, the nervous system and others.

Asthma

Asthma is characterised by a narrowing of the airways leading to breathlessness. Asthma is a complex condition that often needs to be 'controlled' rather than cured. There is a large genetic component which influences who will suffer from this problem. However, it has been hugely on the increase in children in recent decades, which suggests that environmental aspects, including diet, have an important part to play.

Asthma can be terrifying and life threatening and for this reason it is important not to try to self-diagnose and self-treat. A GP's advice should always be sought. As well as taking medical advice, there are other aspects to think about, including avoiding triggers and adjusting diet.

Dietary Help

Addressing some dietary aspects can be very helpful in a number of ways. The overall aim is to reduce the threshold at which 'triggers' have their effect. Helping the body to control inflammation is one important aspect, strengthening the mucus membranes of the respiratory tract is another.

Fish oils Increasing oily fish consumption – as little as once or twice a week – significantly reduces asthma in some children. If eating oily fish such as mackerel, sardines, tuna (fresh), salmon and pink trout is not a likely option, then make sure your child gets a daily fish oil supplement.

Antioxidants Found in fruit and vegetables, these are important for strengthening lung tissue and reducing inflammation and so lowering the number of asthma attacks. Quercitin, a plant flavonoid, found in apples, has been found to be particularly beneficial to lung health. The dark berries including cherries, blueberries, raspberries, blackberries and others are also lung specific. A useful aid is Sambucol, which is European Black Elderberry, available from www.natures store.co.uk

Food Additives Benzoate preservatives (E210–219), sulphur-based food preservatives (E220–228) found in dried fruit, dehydrated vegetables (such as instant potato or packet soup), mushrooms, vinegar, grapes and grape juice, and some artificial food colourings are known to increase the risk of asthma attacks.

Food Sensitivities and Allergies It is fairly common for asthma symptoms to improve when dairy and/or wheat (and sometimes all gluten grains, i.e. wheat, oats, rye and barley) are excluded. If this is the case, then sensible substitutions must be made, such as wholegrain rice and starchy vegetables such as potatoes, or calcium-rich foods and drinks if dairy is being avoided, to make sure a child's diet is not deficient. *See* Food Intolerances, page 82, for more on this.

Avoiding Triggers

There are many well-known triggers that can set off an asthma attack.

Smoking The risk of childhood asthma is increased by parental smoking, even when not in the presence of the child, or being exposed to smoky atmospheres.

Inhaled Allergens House dust mites, animal dander (hair and skin), pollens, mould spores. It is important to identify which might cause problems and eliminate or avoid them. For instance, replacing carpets with hard flooring, curtains with blinds, and using special mattress covers can all make a distinct difference.

Household Products Including sprays, aerosols, air freshners, laundry products. Other irritating gases, such as perfumes and some aromatherapy oils, can also trigger attacks. For natural alternatives to common household chemicals check with your health food shop or read *Talking Dirty with the Queen of Clean* by Linda Cobb. Some of the substitutions are very easy, such as cleaning windows with vinegar instead of using window-cleaning sprays.

Medicines Drugs, including child-formulated medicines (coloured medicine coatings and syrups), aspirin, paracetomol. Speak to your GP.

Atmospheric Changes Including thunderstorms and changes in air temperature (going from warm to cold environments, for example).

Infections Especially upper respiratory tract infections.

Swimming Pools Chloramines result from chlorine reacting with sweat and urine and create a gas. The build up in indoor pools can be considerable (outdoor pools are OK). In one study, they found that children who were susceptible to asthma and who were frequent swimmers had damage to their lungs that was equivalent to adult smokers.

Exercise Gentle exercise is beneficial, particularly swimming (though see above), but vigorous exercise can bring on attacks.

Emotional Stress In children it is common to have attacks when parents are arguing.

Other Help

Herbal Helpers

- Camomile is soothing for asthmatics and can be drunk as a tea.
- Galeops, or Hemp Nettle, supports lung health by replacing silica needed in the lungs and trachea, and the silicic acid it contains supports immune health. Available from Bioforce (01294 277 344) or www.bioforce.co.uk
- Liquorice has a similar structure to cortisone and has an anti-inflammatory action (the sweets have an effect but as they are sugary can be counterproductive, so we are talking about the herb liquorice root). The cortisone steroid effect is more gentle than that of medication and does not suppress the immune system in the long run.
- Children should not take herbs without the advice of a medical herbalist, especially with regard to how they might interact with prescribed medication (*see* page XXX for Medical Herbalist information). You should not stop prescribed medication.

Breathing Exercises

The Buteyko method of shallow breathing has been shown in studies to help asthmatics. Their Breathology Programme is easy to follow from a video or workshop. Children from four years and older can follow the method taught to adults as they have the control, coordination and attention span needed. Younger children are encouraged to adopt the measures through play. For more, go to www.freedom fromasthma.com

See also Peanut and Other Allergies, page 195.

Ear Infections

Otitis media, or glue ear, is when the middle ear becomes inflamed and filled with mucus. It can be severe enough to impair hearing. Recurrent ear infections in children must be taken seriously and properly diagnosed by your GP. Antibiotics are often prescribed. If the glue ear presents a real problem it is frequently advised that grommets are inserted in a small, but still anxiety provoking, operation to open up the ear canal.

Yet it is relatively easy to reduce the number of ear infections a child suffers, or to pretty much eliminate them, by improving immune health and dealing with any food intolerances to which a child might be prone. Dealing with an ear infection in the early stages by using a swab of tea tree oil – soak a cotton bud and very gently wipe inside the ear canal, being careful not to probe too deep – two or three times daily when earache first sets in, can be an effective way to stop it in its tracks before medication is needed. Tea tree is a potent anti-bacterial agent, which does not promote antibiotic resistance. If sinuses are blocked then inhaling steam over a sink can help to loosen mucus (but take care not to scald).

It is often the case that children with glue ear consume far too much sugar, which suppresses the immune system, are prone to dairy allergy or intolerance, which encourages mucus build up, or have some other food intolerance, such as a sensitivity to wheat. A trial period for a month, eliminating dietary suspects, will give a good indication of the solution. With dairy or wheat foods it is important to make sensible substitutions so that the child's diet is not deficient in any way (see Food Intolerances, page 82). If your child is very attached to a particular food you may find it easier to reduce dependency slowly. To give the exercise a fair run, however, the month of eliminating the food or foods must start from the point where you manage to eliminate it completely.

One study has found that children who were prone to ear infections experienced a reduced need for antibiotics of two-thirds, or no need for medication at all, when they took cod liver oil on a daily basis (I would recommend fish oils supplements rather than cod liver oil).

Eczema

Eczema is a dry skin condition, which at its most severe erupts in wet pustules. There are two main types of eczema, contact and atopic.

As the name suggests, contact eczema (also called dermatitis) is triggered by contact with something to which the child is allergic. Suspicion could, for instance, fall on, washing powder, particular fabrics (on toys as well as clothing), latex rubber, sticking plasters, perfumes, a plant or chlorine in pools. Surprisingly, peanut oil is in the formula of some creams, including nappy creams and even eczema creams prescribed by GPs, and this can make the condition much worse. You need to double-check this.

Atopic eczema has a genetic link, involves a sensitivity to common environmental factors, and it is much more difficult to find a specific cause. Commonly, atopic eczema involves an allergy to house dust mites. Certain foods can be another trigger. It can also be triggered by stressful events. The condition typically starts before a child is four years old.

It is common for eczema to develop when moving from breast milk to cow's milk. Soya should also be suspect, as it is often used instead of cow's milk, and yet 25 per cent of cow's milk intolerant children also have a problem with soya. Other common triggers are eggs, oranges and wheat. Carefully following an elimination period where these foods are avoided and re-introduced can give a clear indication of whether or not they are involved. This is not always easy, however, and care needs to be taken to be strict about following this. If it is found that a particular food or foods need to be avoided it is important to make substitutions which mean that your child will not end up missing out nutritionally. If oranges are to be avoided, it is fine as long as other fruit are consumed. If wheat is avoided then add, for instance, oats, rice and rye into the diet. *See* Food Intolerances, page 82.

Atopic children who are troubled by eczema often do not metabolise fatty acids properly, or simply do not get enough of them in the diet. Piercing a capsule of evening primrose oil and gently smoothing the contents on the inflamed skin can help. Make sure your child gets 1–3 teaspoons of flax oil daily (depending on the size/age of your child). It is non-toxic, so you can't overdose and you need to get sufficient into your child to make a difference. Add it to food – to soups, smoothies, salads or vegetables – but do not cook with it as this destroys its beneficial properties. Maintaining this for at least 6–8 weeks usually makes a wonderful difference. Eating a couple of portions of oily fish a week is also very beneficial. Oily fish include mackerel, sardines, fresh tuna, salmon, sprats and pink trout.

Nutrients that are important for general skin health, and so help to repair skin, are zinc and vitamin A. Zinc is found in all protein foods, including fish, lean meat, eggs, pulses, seeds and nuts. Vitamin A is made in the body from beta-carotene, which is found in orange and dark green produce, including carrots, apricots, cantaloupe melons and spinach.

The majority of cases of childhood eczema also involve the anti-biotic resistant 'superbug' *Staphylococcus aureus* (SA) and it could be the toxin produced by this bacteria on the infected skin which is causing the problem. Manuka honey is effective against SA and can make a soothing topical ointment, though it is sticky! Honey is also hydrating for skin – leave it on for ten minutes at a time.

Steroid creams are often prescribed and they can certainly be useful when in a crisis and you have a child who is itching and in discomfort. However, ultimately, they do not solve the root of the problem and can also lead to slight thining of the skin. Adding a handful of oats or camomile tea bags to a bath can be very soothing. An oat-based cream which has been very effective in trials for children with eczema is Oatmilk Treatment Cream from Aderma (call 0845 1170116 for stockists).

As with any dry skin condition it is also helpful to maintain good daily water intake to avoid dehydration.

See also Peanut and Other Allergies, page 195.

Hay Fever

Hay fever is a seasonal allergy to pollens and it affects about one in six children from the age of five. Itchy, watery eyes, streaming and blocked noses, tight throats, sneezing and headaches are all symptoms. Rising pollution levels and house dust mites worsen the condition. It is common for asthma to co-exist with hay fever. The difference between hay fever and rhinitis is that hay fever is strictly seasonal while rhinitis results from nasal allergy symptoms all year round.

The usual advice for hay fever is to stay indoors at peak pollen times and to take antihistamines when affected. The sensitivity could be to tree pollen if it is earlier in the year, grasses and weeds mid-season and moulds and fungus spores late-season. As we are having milder winters the season is now longer than it was 30 years ago.

One simple barrier method that can help is to apply a little Vaseline to the inside of the nostrils. By creating a barrier between pollen and the mucus membranes of the nasal passages this can reduce symptoms. Obviously be careful and gentle and do not go too high inside the nose.

Some children respond well to reducing the amount of dairy products and/or wheat-based products in their diet during the hay fever season. It is possible that they are linked because ruminants (cows, goats and sheep) feed on grass, to which wheat is related, and the dairy may harbour allergens. Dairy products also tend to have the effect of making susceptible people produce more nasal mucus. Dairy includes milk, cheese and yoghurt (though yoghurt is often tolerated). Wheat-based foods include bread, pasta, cake, pastry and cereals. Oats and rye are also sometimes a problem. Other grains, such as rice, buckwheat and millet, and starches, such as potatoes and yams, are usually fine. Occasionally, there is a sensitivity to legumes, including soya, peanuts, lentils and other pulses.

A favourite nutritional tactic is a supplement of quercitin (a plant bioflavonoid found in apples and onions) with vitamin C, which are natural antihistamines, taken during the season. It is suitable from age three onwards and is available from Solgar in independent health food shops or from www.solgar.com

Camomile has anti-allergy properties, while plantain is anti-allergy, anti-catarrhal and acts as a tonic for the mucus membranes of the respiratory tract. Plantain and Camomile drops for children are available from Napiers herbalists (0131 343 6683 or www.napiers.net). Soothing lotions for itchy eyes include cucumber slices rubbed over closed eyes, rosewater-steeped cotton pads and cold, used, tea-bags placed over the eyes for 5 minutes.

Headaches

Regular headaches in children should always be taken seriously, particularly if they start up suddenly. A doctor will rule out any potentially serious causes, as well as more mundane possible causes such as inflamed sinuses. In many cases it is also helpful to rule out causes such as stresses and strains around the neck area – a visit to a osteopath or chiropracter might be advisable. You may also need to visit your dentist to check out any problems relating to teeth grinding or jaw tension.

It is common for the parents of children who regularly take pain relieving medication such as paracetamol to find that the medicine is contributing to the headaches and causing a 'rebound' effect. In these cases it is suspected that the liver is not able to process the medication adequately and so compounds circulate, which worsens the headache.

Migraines are different to headaches in their cause, but are often lumped together and may be difficult to differentiate in children.

Children often experience migraines in different ways to adults. They commonly get stomachaches, feel nauseous and even vomit.

The most common dietary cause of headaches and migraines is blood sugar imbalance, which comes from not eating regular meals and snacks, or from eating meals and snacks consisting of too much sugar or refined carbohydrates. This causes peaks and troughs in the blood sugar supply to the brain. Other possible dietary causes can be investigated once you are sure you have got the frequency and type of meals and snacks resolved. See page 169 for suggestions of healthy snacks.

Migraines are sometimes triggered by foods that are either not metabolised by that child, or those which cause a reaction due to an intolerance of some other sort. The artificial sweetener aspartame is found in many foods aimed at children, such as yoghurts, desserts, sweets and fruit drinks, and this can cause adverse reactions. Other foods that might lead to headaches or migraines due to the presence of compounds called amines, include chocolate, oranges, pickles, mature cheeses, Marmite, smoked sausage, Horlicks, broad beans, pickled herrings, canned figs and overripe avocadoes. Nitrate or nitrite containing foods such a sausages, bacon, salamis and frankfurters can also trigger migraines. Sensitivities are not likely to all of these foods all at the same time, but children can find that particular foods do not agree with them.

Foods to which there may be an intolerance, and which can promote a build up of mucus in sinuses, or other less definable reactions, include dairy products and wheat products. If all else fails then it is often worth ruling out food intolerances. It can also be a great help to include oily fish, or fish oil supplements, which are rich in the omega-3 oils that can help to regulate migraines. Magnesium deficiency is also often involved in both headaches and migraines and foods rich in this mineral include all green leafy vegetables, dried fruit, nuts, seeds, whole grains and soyabeans.

Camomile is very soothing to drink and lavender is the classic anti-headache aromatherapy treatment. Other herbs that can help with migraines are feverfew and butterbur (petasites), but these are only suitable for older children in their mid- to late-teens.

Food Intolerances

Food intolerances are different to food allergies. An allergy will usually be acute and show itself very soon after a food has been eaten. It always involves an immune system response. *See* Peanut and Other Allergies, page 195, for more on this.

A food intolerance sometimes involves the immune system, sometimes involves an inability to process a constituent of a food (usually due to an enzyme deficiency), or may involve a response that is not fully understood (this accounts for a number of intolerance-type reactions). There are also straightforward food aversions, where a particular food is simply disliked to the point where it causes nausea.

Food intolerances can contribute to a number of adverse symptoms (*see* box). The most common food intolerances are:

- Milk and dairy products.
- Wheat (including bread, pastry, pasta).
- Other common foods that cause intolerances are soya, eggs, oats and corn.

Symptoms that can be Linked to Food Intolerance

- Asthma
- Catarrh
- Dark eye circles
- Ear infections
- Frequent infections
- Listlessness and low energy
- Wind
- Bloating
- Constipation
- Diarrhoea
- Eczema
- Headaches and migraines
- Nausea
- Rashes

In order to work out if your child is intolerant to a food:

- First arm yourself with all the information you need. Become familiar with foods that might be causing a problem and familiarise yourself with suitable substitutes. This will probably involve a trip to a supermarket or your local health food shop to see which products fit your needs.
- Choose a quiet couple of weeks in which you can experiment. It may be better not to do this during term time when it may be awkward to navigate round school meals and lunch boxes.
- Explain to your child what you are doing, why and how. It is important to get his cooperation and willingness to proceed. If a child is troubled by symptoms then he should be motivated to see if a resolution can be found.
- Make a plan together as far as you are able (this is age dependant).
- Stock up the larder and fridge with a wide selection of tasty goodies that will not be detrimental to the project.
- Avoid whichever food or foods you have decided on for a period of 10–14 days. See if symptoms improve. Of course it is important that these should be symptoms which would normally have occurred in this time frame and not, say, once monthly.
- Keep a diary of all adverse reactions, benefits, changes in symptoms and new symptoms.
- Reintroduce the food after the exclusion period in an amount that would normally be eaten (i.e. a slice of bread or a small bowl of cereal). See what happens. If symptoms return anything up to 36 hours later then you probably have your answer.
- It may be a threshold problem where, for example, one slice of bread does not cause problems, but three or four slices over a daytime does.

Substitutions for Common Foods that Cause Intolerance

Milk and dairy See the section on page 162.

Wheat Look for foods made from oats, rye, barley, corn, rice, quinoa, buckwheat (not wheat despite the name), millet, potato, sweet potato, chestnut flour, sago, tapioca, lentil flour (popadoms) and chickpea flour (gram flour). Familiar foods such as pasta and crackers are available in many of these grains and make easy substitutions. However, if a product is called, say, oatcakes, still check the small print in case wheat flour is also included. For some children it is not sufficient to avoid just wheat flour, other gluten grains need to be avoided too. These are rye and barley, and sometimes also oats.

Eggs These are found in many processed foods and you need to read the labels to check, though they will not always be declared if only a small amount is used. Egg-free mayonnaise is available from health food shops. At home you can use cornflour or arrowroot in place of egg for thickening, milk or soya milk for glazing when baking, tomato purée or mashed potato for binding, and bicarbonate of soda or cream of tartar as raising agents instead of eggs when baking.

Soya Again, this is finding its way into many packaged and processed foods, including most breads and many cakes. You can also find it described as TVP (textured vegetable protein).

It is extremely important not to continue with avoiding a staple food or group of foods in a child for long without working out a good list of substitutions and getting used to using them regularly. It is vital that a child's diet should not be unnecessarily restricted to avoid the risk of losing out on important nutrients. Large supermarkets are increasingly aware of this need and have 'free-from' labelling, special dietary requirement sections and list of products which fulfil certain needs available if you ask the store manager.

A small number of parents become so involved with their child's symptoms and health that they develop a distorted view of the subject. The anxiety levels alone are probably enough to ensure that their child is reacting adversely. If you feel that you are getting confused on the subject or cannot interpret your child's symptoms adequately please see your doctor or seek other suitable professional help, such as from a nutritionist who specialises in paediatric work.

Generally, it is not too difficult to manage a food intolerance, as long as you are informed and prepared. It is easier to think about what you can prepare rather than what can't be eaten. So, for instance, if wheat and dairy are being avoided together you can centre meals on meat, eggs (these are not dairy), fish, pulses, fruits and vegetables, rice, potatoes, oats and rye. With a positive list such as this it is easy to see how tasty meals can be served with little trouble. As there are so many good substitutions for dairy foods these days, including soya, oat and rice milks, yoghurts and desserts, finding alternatives is not usually a problem.

The main difficulty seems to be bread-textured foods. You can use crackers such as oatcakes, rye crackers and rice cakes, and non-wheat cereals such as rice puffs, corn flakes and porridge, but sometimes a slice of bread would make life easier. Gluten-free bread is available but can be uninteresting. Good gluten-free flours from Buxton Foods/Stamp Foods for making your own bread are available from large supermarkets.

Wheat- and Dairy-Free Baking Recipes

These are some easy things to make at home.

Pancakes Choose your favourite recipe and just substitute rice flour and soya milk for flour and milk. Put 1 egg, 75 ml soya milk, 2 or 3 tablespoons of rice flour (depending on how runny you want the mixture) in a blender or food processor. Blend for a few seconds. Melt a scraping of butter in a frying pan and, when hot, pour in half the mixture. When the pancake sets, turn it over with a spatula. Make a second pancake with the remaining mixture. Top the pancakes with banana, blueberries and Greek yoghurt or any other sweet or savoury topping your child fancies.

Blinis Blinis are a good standby instead of bread and can be used, say, for eggs on toast or with nut butter and jam. If you increase the quantities, you can make loads of them and then store them in the freezer, interleaved with greaseproof paper. When you need one, just pop it in the toaster or under the grill to warm through. They are usually made with sour yoghurt and yeast to lighten them, but they can be made more quickly as follows. Make as for the pancake recipe above, but use buckwheat flour instead of rice flour. This gives the blinis their characteristic slightly sour taste. Blinis are made smaller than pancakes – $1^1/_2$ tablespoons of mix makes a blini about 12 cm across.

Corn Muffins Preheat the oven to 190ºC. Mix together 125 g yellow cornmeal, 50 g ground almonds, $1^1/_2$ teaspoons bicarbonate of soda and a large pinch of salt in a bowl. In a large jug, beat together 2 eggs, 100 ml soya milk and 2 tablespoons walnut oil. Pour this liquid over the dry ingredients and mix together well. Spoon the mixture into greased muffin tins and bake for about 20 minutes until golden and firm to the touch. Allow to cool slightly before eating – they are best served warm with a little butter. Any muffins you don't eat will keep for a couple of days in an airtight tin. Makes 8–10 muffins.

Flapjacks Melt 100 g unsalted butter, 25 g maple syrup and 25 g brown sugar over a low heat. Add 75 g finely chopped dates/apricots/currants (choose one or two of these). Mix in 200 g porridge oats and 50 g desiccated coconut, and stir until well mixed. Press into a 9" baking tin/flat dish and bake in a medium oven for 15 minutes. Allow to cool in the tin before cutting into squares.

Muesli To make a wheat-free muesli just combine several flaked grains such as raw oats, millet flakes and buckwheat flakes in a large, wide-necked jar. In separate jars keep some (or all) of the following: sliced almonds, walnut pieces, sunflower seeds, pine nuts, coconut flakes, raisins, chopped dried apricots, chopped dried dates. Your child can make up his own selection to turn it into delicious muesli. Soak with apple or orange juice or soya or rice milk, and chop or grate some fresh fruit on top.

Fruit and Vegetables

There is nothing insignificant about eating fruit and vegetables. If you think about our muscley cousins the gorillas, who live on a diet which is largely fruit-based you will realise that they can build strong healthy individuals. This is one of the most important health gifts we can give our children.

And does an apple a day really keep the doctor away? The answer is yes. A recent study showed that an apple a day improves lung function significantly, probably because of an antioxidant compound found in apples called quercitin, and this is the sort of information which could be really useful for parents of children with, for instance, asthma. Fruits and vegetables are packed with vitamins, minerals, antioxidant compounds, fibre for bowel health, water and sugars which the body metabolises slowly for a steady energy supply. The fructose in fruit has a steadying effect on blood sugar levels and does not have the jarring effect on the body that table and confectionery sugar (sucrose) has. Glucose, when it comes from fruit, is useful as a readily available source of energy because it has fibre with it to ease the effect on blood sugar balance.

Vegetables are probably even more important than fruit and while it is fairly easy to get kids to eat fruit, encouraging a taste for vegetables could be even more important for overall health. Compounds in vegetables are believed to be of vital importance in preventing all the major degenerative diseases such as cancer, heart disease and strokes. Vegetables are also important for bone health as they contain magnesium, which is needed to balance out calcium, and green leafy vegetables are one of the best sources of folic acid.

Antioxidants are protective for us because they stop damage to our body tissues. You can see oxidation damage happening if you cut an apple in half and watch it turn brown. If you sprinkle lemon juice on it, which is rich in the antioxidant vitamin C, this limits the degeneration and keeps the apple flesh white. Antioxidants have, more or less, the same effect inside our bodies, and those of our children.

How Much is a Portion?

We are advised to eat a minimum of five portions of fruits and vegetables a day.

- A total of 400 g a day is the aim for adults, which means that a portion is 80 g (3oz).
- One portion is equivalent to any of the following: 1 apple, 1 orange, 1 banana, 1 peach, 2 small kiwis, 2 plums, 1 large slice of pineapple or melon, a generous handful of strawberries or grapes or 2 tablespoons of fruit salad.
- In vegetable terms, a portion means 2 tablespoons of veg or beans or one small dessert bowl of salad.

- A wine-glass of fruit or vegetable juice also counts as a portion (but only once a day).
- Eating fresh, frozen, dried or juiced fruit and vegetables, as well as those cooked into dishes (such as pies) all count. Canned fruit and vegetables also count (though, with a few exceptions, I like them less, personally).
- There are no guidelines for children, but one age-adjusted size that is often used is to say a portion is a handful and obviously children have smaller hands than adults.
- Eating more than five portions is of even more benefit and, optimistically, it looks like the guidelines could be revised upwards in the future to seven or eight portions daily, as it already has been in the United States.

But These Don't Count

Unfortunately the following don't have enough fruit in them to count as a portion, no matter how much your child wishes it:

- A glass of squash or 'juice drink' (but a glass of 100 per cent juice does).
- A fruit yoghurt, fruit and nut chocolate bar or fruit jam (but dried fruit, fresh fruit added to yoghurt or fruit dunked in chocolate does).
- Tomato ketchup (but slices of tomato or grilled tomatoes do, as does tomato pasta sauce)
- Also, while potatoes do provide vitamin C they do not count as a portion of vegetable as they are counted as a starchy food (along with rice and bread).

These are a couple of worrying statistics:

- Less than one in five children get the recommended five portions of fruit and vegetables daily.
- Fruit dropped from 5th place to 13th in a recent survey of children's favourite desserts.

If your child is refusing fruits and vegetables, aim to work out why. Children usually like sweet fruits but if they have easy access to lots of sweeter snacks, confectionery and puddings, these will inevitably win hands down. The parents themselves may not set an example by eating fruits or vegetables. Another possible explanation is that the choice of fruit and vegetables on offer is not interesting enough and the child is simply getting bored. You can improve their interest in fruits and vegetables by getting them involved with preparation, cooking and storing – and, if you live in a rural area, in cultivation.

Serving Ideas for Fruits and Vegetables
- Vegetable suggestions that are child-friendly include peas, baked beans, green beans, broccoli and cauliflower cheese, carrot and cucumber fingers, 'Popeye' spinach, cowboy black-eyed beans, baby sweetcorn, mini-carrots, sweet tasting roasted red and yellow peppers or home-made vegetable soups.
- Pasta with tomato pesto, steamed broccoli or asparagus dunked in olive oil or sauces and sweet carrot sticks with dips are all popular with most kids.
- Dried fruit such as raisins, apple rings, apricots or prunes are often enjoyed as a snack or added to cereals or puddings by even the most fussy fruit-avoiding child.
- Raw vegetable sticks are often eaten when cooked vegetables are refused.
- Small portions of a variety of vegetables, or mixed vegetables, instead of great big hunks of one veg are often more appealing.

- By the same token cut up fruit often wins over whole fruit.
- Few children will turn down a really thick and yummy milk shake or smoothie made with fresh fruit. Experiment with banana, strawberries, peach, pear, mango, melon, watermelon or papaya – just add one or two of these to a glass of milk, juice or water in the blender and whizz it up in seconds. For variety, add in a little coconut milk (but not too much as it is very rich).
- Another idea is to whizz some berries (fresh, frozen or canned without sugar or syrup) in a blender for an instant sauce to go on top of ice cream.
- You can successfully serve vegetables which are usually turned down by incorporating them into curries or pasta sauces.
- Baked apple or baked banana are delicious and easy.
- Five portions does not mean five 'hunks' and could mean, for instance, a portion of apple crumble. Most children enjoy a crumble, cobbler or pie made with lots of fresh stewed apples, berries or plums (experiment to see how little sugar you can get away with). For ideas on how to incorporate fruit into puddings *see* Desserts, page 42.
- Dried fruit are even more nutritious than fresh fruit in terms of their antioxidant value with, for instance, prunes having six times the value of plums, and raisins being similarly high when compared to grapes. Dried fruit are concentrated sources of sugar, however, so you may want to serve them alongside other foods.
- Remember to include a portion of fruit or vegetable with each breakfast so you only have four more to think about during the rest of the day. *See* Breakfast, page 27.
- Next time you bake fairy cakes with your child put some fruit in the bottom of the tin, add the cake mixture on top, and make little 'up-side-down' cakes.
- If you tend to serve meals based on 'meat and two veg' think about meals that are 'composite meals' and include vegetables in the ingredients – for instance, stews, curries, chilli, pies and omelettes.

- A great success with children is fruit dipped in melted chocolate (the best option is good quality dark chocolate – which is also, incidentally, high in antioxidants). This can either be served as a chocolate fondue or can be put in the fridge for the chocolate to harden around the fruit. Strawberries, grapes, cubes of melon and banana slices are all delicious served in this way.

- Frozen fruit and vegetables are just as good as fresh and help to extend the season.

- Canned fruit is usually a poor relative, as the canning process is so heat intensive that a certain amount of the vitality of fruit (vitamins and enzymes) will have been destroyed. The exception that proves the rule (there is always one!) are canned purple and red fruits, which are still rich in the antioxidant proanthocyanidins, so stocking up on canned blueberries, blackberries and raspberries can help to carry you through the winter months and are a useful addition to baking recipes. Avoid fruits canned in syrups or sugar.

- Canned vegetables do not, in my opinion, have as nice a consistency or flavour as fresh or frozen. However, technically, they do count as a portion of veg. Canned tomatoes, in particular, are good sources of the antioxidant compound lycopene and the beta-carotene in canned carrots is very absorbable. Most canned vegetables will need to have the salty water they are canned in drained or rinsed off.

Good Food Fun

I have never been one of the funny-face-pizza brigade. Life just seems to be a little too busy for this. However, there is no doubt that children enjoy this approach and us adults have to, sometimes, gracefully give in. And so cakes are built into trains, smiley face sandwiches are constructed and watercress soup (with a wisp of yoghurt) gets renamed green dragon soup (with a wisp of smoke). Halved baked potatoes are dressed up with peas, baby sweetcorn and strips of pepper to make dancing funny-men faces with curly parsley hair, and dough 'sausages' are wound round on the baking tray and dressed up with tomato, ham and olive halves before baking to make pizza snakes. And if your imagination runs out, there are many children's cookery books in the children's craft section of your local library to give you ideas, and some fun suggestions are included in Lunchbox Planning, page 147.

However there is more to making food fun than just this. It is all about having a family culture of enjoying food. Here's a little quiz:

which of these two groups of statements rings most true to you and
your family?:

- Food is fun; Food is delicious; Food is interesting; Eating with
  family and friends is convivial; Discovering new cuisines is an
  adventure.
- Shopping for food is a bore; Food preparation is a chore; Eating
  is something to be got out of the way; I avoid ingredients I don't
  know how to cook as I might mess them up.

While the second group of statements is true for most of us some of
the time, if this is the general way you feel about food this could be
a problem for encouraging good nutrition in your child. One of the
main themes of this book is to encourage the former group of statements more often than not.

There is one essential principle to concentrate on: Putting good
food – nutritious food – higher up the priority list. Do this one thing
and the rest will follow. This does not mean becoming obsessed by
food and nutrition, nor does it mean faddy diets or complicated allergy
regimes. There may be times when taking a therapeutic approach to
food and health is appropriate, but, by and large, particularly with
children, having a rounded approach to enjoying food is the one which
will win through and pay dividends.

Making good food fun is more important that it might seem at first.
Healthiness is an abstract idea for children, but fun is not abstract,
and nor is food. One survey looked at cultural influences on how the
attitude of mothers affected their children's view of eating and health.
UK mums, without realising it, promoted guilt-ridden ideas of what
foods are healthy and which are not as a result of their own attitudes
towards dieting and in their explanations of what constituted healthy
eating. Italian mums, on the other hand, conveyed their own pleasure
at cooking and in so doing instilled a positive attitude in their children towards eating and its link to health. They actively involved their
children in discovering new foods, and in food education.

The way you encourage appreciation of good food, and make good food fun is to:

- Encourage your children to learn about cooking.
- Eat as a family.
- Take an interest in how dishes are made and discuss ingredients.
- Plan meals together.
- Take your children to real restaurants to eat real food, and read the menus together, instead of to fast-food outlets.
- Find out where food comes from (i.e. the soil, not the supermarket).
- If funny faces is what it takes, then fine, but also don't forget that presenting food attractively always makes eating more of a pleasure.

See also Kids in the Kitchen, page 121, Slow Food, page 221, and Holiday Eating, page 99.

Growth and Height

While it is important to keep a check on your child's growth, it is equally important not to become over-anxious about it. Children grow in fits and starts. However, if your child is not growing for an extended length of time, say three months or more, nor putting on weight, then you may need to discuss the situation with your doctor or health visitor. Height and weight are measured on centile charts which are available from your health visitor.

Making sure that calorie intake is sufficient is obviously important. It is common for health-conscious parents to give their children low-fat milk and high-fibre bran cereals, which is not really appropriate. Children have high nutrient requirements per kilogram of body weight compared to adults and a small appetite may mean a child is not getting all the nutrients he needs. Zinc- and iron-rich foods are needed for optimum growth and mental performance and yet large numbers of children are deficient in these two nutrients. If your child is not a meat eater (a good source of these nutrients), offer them instead eggs, cheese, baked beans, wholegrains and snacks such as nuts and popcorn. Drinking a small glass of orange juice with meals will improve iron absorption from plant sources.

Estimated Average Requirements for Energy (Kcals)

(Varies depending on activity levels.)

	Boys	Girls
1–3 years	1250	1150
4–6 years	1700	1550
7–10 years	2000	1750
11–14 years	2200	1850
15–18 years	2750	2100

*These figures have been round up or down.
Kcals=Kilocalories (commonly called calories).

It is worth writing a food diary for four days and working out if your child is getting the required number of calories (four days gives a better picture than a day, just divide the total by four). If necessary you can cram the calories in, where possible, with higher calorie foods such as full-fat dairy products, avocado, nut butters, nuts and seeds. If your child is filling up on cordials and squashes this can blunt his appetite at meal times. It could be appropriate to give a child formulated multi-vitamin and mineral supplement.

While obesity has hit the headlines as the major health concern facing today's children, at the other end of the scale are children who are picky eaters and who do not appear to be eating enough to maintain growth. One study found that 50 per cent of children who were checking in to a hospital's A&E department were undernourished in

What to Do If You Are Worried About Your Child's Growth

- If you are worried about whether your child is eating enough it is not only loss of weight but also lack of growth or increasing weight that you need to look for. It is common to lose weight in the short term when ill. However, children need to be growing, so if their weight is static or they are losing weight over a period of 3–6 months then it is a cause for concern. A sustained fall through 2 centile spaces justifies a more detailed assessment. Children often cross through one centile space during the first year.
- Consult your doctor or health visitor/dietician/paediatrician if you are concerned (to exclude coeliacs disease in the underweight, or hormonal abnormalities, for instance).
- Snacking on low-nutrient foods which displace healthier foods is a frequent cause of poor appetite and nutrient intake. Sugary cordials, squashes, colas and juices are the worst offenders. Too much milk can also reduce appetite and displace meals resulting in poor nutrient levels. See Appetite Squashers, page 10. Offer water instead.

some way. We are also seeing a worrying increase in anorexia in children as young as eight. Undernourishment can lead to developmental delays (physical, language, behaviour and intellectual) and impaired immune health.

Holiday Eating

If you play it right, holidays are the perfect time to encourage your child to be more adventurous with food by sampling local fare. Apart from having the advantage of widening horizons, you will find it a lot easier if, when in Rome, your children eat as the Romans do. Worrying about finding restaurants that serve the British child's staples of chicken nuggets or sausages can put a damper on a holiday. There are many areas in which the average British child's diet is limited, or overly dependent on certain things, such as fizzy drinks. A holiday is the ideal time to break the mould.

- Children in continental Europe tend to eat a wider range of foods, which is an ideal way of ensuring a balanced diet and range of nutrients.
- Children particularly like seeing the choice they are going to make. This makes mezze, antipasto, hors d'oeuvre and smorgasbords very popular.

- Mediterranean and Scandinavian food is terrific for introducing more oily fish, which are rich in the omega-3 fats that are needed for nerve functioning. Seafood is also rich in selenium, which is great for balancing moods.

- A holiday can be the ideal time to eat more fresh fruits and vegetables, especially in hot countries. Rich in antioxidant compounds and fibre, they are vital for immune health.

- Beans and pulses are creatively presented in Latin countries and are excellent sources of fibre for digestive health.

- Even in the United States food can be entirely regional: Creole food, such as gumbo (stew), in New Orleans; clam chowder in New England; 'Dutch food' (really German – deutsche) in Pennsylvania; black-eyed beans (cowboy food) and Tex-Mex in the border states; hush puppies (deep-fried batter balls), collards (greens) and fried fish (or even 'gator') in the South; and Pacific rim (loads of delicately presented seafood) in California. Wherever you are, make a point of seeking out the regional options for a more specific taste experience instead of falling into the hamburger trap. New York is such a melting pot that every cuisine is on offer – Jewish, Middle Eastern, Chinese, Japanese, Vietnamese – what an adventure! By far the biggest problem is likely to be one of huge choice and even huger portions.

- Children may be put off by strong smells or tastes. Having said this, they can be unexpectedly adventurous when it comes to foods such as anchovies and olives and it is a good idea to have an agreement that they taste everything at least once. Avoid putting them off with your own dislikes, prejudices and expectations and you may be surprised.

Getting into the Groove

- Before going on holiday, make a project of discovering what the gastronomic possibilities are. For instance, have a French day with croissants for breakfast, baguettes and fromage for lunch and a cassoulet for supper; or a German day with weiner sausages, sauerkraut and dumplings.

- Take your children on a virtual gastronomic tour by visiting some of the tourist websites that discuss food. Some that I found were:

  www.travel-guide.com

  www.bbc.co.uk/education/languages/spanish/lj/

  cultural-notes/regional_cooking.shtml

  www.cs.umd.edu/users/kandogan/FTA/TurkishCuisine/

  cuisine.html

  www.deliciousitaly.com

  http://cityguide.se/malmo/tourism/?lang=en;article=scaniafood

- Visit your local library and take out cookery books for your children to see what is in store.

- Encourage your children to observe local children eating local fare.

- Lead by example. Your children can become more adventurous by tasting some of the food from your plate.

- Enjoy shopping forays to local markets spilling over with local specialities, and include your children in selecting produce and choosing the menu.

But Be Cautious

Some of the most authentic and delicious food adventures can be had from road-side vendors, but be warned that hygiene is often not all it might be and you could be playing Russian roulette with food poisoning. On the other hand, nothing beats the experience of fresh sardines with local tomatoes from a shack on a Portuguese beach, fragrant chickpeas from a vendor in Turkey or watermelon from the roadside in Florida, so you may want to take your chances!

Whilst it is not something to totally rely upon, a course of beneficial bacteria and/or prebiotics for three or four weeks before you go on holiday can reduce the risk of a bad reaction to food poisoning. This is very effective at reducing the incidence rate and seriousness of a food poisoning attack. The beneficial bacteria colonise the gut and literally crowd out the pathogenic bacteria which make you ill. *See* Diarrhoea, page 242, for more information.

Beware of food that might be perishable and not properly refrigerated, such as shellfish or food left out on a countertop in the heat. One way of assessing the situation is to see what the locals are eating because, as regular customers, they are often given first choice of the best produce (this may sound cynical but is often true).

Home Remedy Kit

Parents often prefer to have the choice of some effective home remedies. It is always important to get correct diagnoses from your doctor, and medication is often necessary. There are times, however, when non-toxic remedies are appropriate for children. These are some ideas:

Bicarbonate of soda The chemical in stings is mostly formic acid and a paste of bicarbonate of soda, which is alkaline, applied to the puncture wound neutralises the acid causing the pain. (In countries with regular jelly fish problems a little urine is used for the same effect, when bicarbonate of soda is not to hand, though I couldn't possibly recommend this!)

Calendula A calendula cream is gentle and soothing and is ideal for nappy rash, skin rashes, bites and burns. A calendula infusion can be made to rinse hair and get rid of dandruff.

Camomile Tea bags infused in a bath (or a handful of oats added to bathwater) helps soothe itchy skin conditions such as eczema, sunburn and nettle rash.

Chickweed Cream For very itchy skin inflammations such as stings and nettle rash.

Chocolate This triggers endorphins in the brain, which help to subdue pain – a quick cube of chocolate in the mouth works wonders after a bee sting or just before an injection!

Citronella A pleasant-smelling insect repellent available in candles, as an alternative to chemical deterrents.

Echinacea Use a children's formulation of this wonderful herb for boosting the immune system and keeping winter bugs at bay.

Fennel Oil A couple of drops in warm water with honey soothes coughs and bronchitis. It is an ingredient in classic gripe water and also helps to relieve stomach cramps.

Flaxseeds A daily teaspoon of ground seeds sprinkled on to breakfast cereal or in a smoothie will help to gently ease constipation.

Green Clay Or Bentonite or Fuller's Earth, available from your chemist, mixed to a paste and applied to wounds such as a sting and allowed to dry is soothing, as is camomile lotion. It is a very effective poultice for infected wounds after applying an antibacterial such as tea tree oil.

Geranium A sweet-smelling insect repellent moisturising lotion, based on geranium, lavender and melissa, is available from Alfresco (020 8348 6704 or www.alfresco.uk.com).

Herbal Anti-Headlice Shampoo Much better than using pharma-ceutical chemical-based shampoos which use organophosphates. My favourites are Chinese Whispers, available from health food shops or www.naturesstore.co.uk, or Nitty Gritty (020 7460 0166 or www.nittygritty.co.uk).

Ice Cubes Apply a cube of ice, or small bag of peas, wrapped in tissue or a thin towel to help to numb the area of an insect bite or sting or bring down any swelling.

Lavender Essential Oil Applied topically, it can help to soothe and reduce the itch and inflammation of stings (avoid the eye area).

Manuka Honey A potent antibacterial and antiviral agent, this honey has been used very effectively in hospitals to treat open wounds. It has even been shown to be effective against the antibiotic resistant MRSA bug. Used with lemon and hot water it makes a soothing drink for sore throats. Manuka honey can inhibit the streptococcal bug, plus it slips down easily and is comforting. Available from Comvita (www.comvita.com).

Neem Oil An insect repellent, it discourages mosquitos and other insects and also acts as a balm if they do bite. It is a traditional Indian remedy, where trees are planted outside houses, but it has a strongish smell. Available from Bioforce (01294 277 344 or www.bioforce.co.uk).

Oregano Oil Expensive (don't be fobbed off with marjoram masquerading as oregano), it can be dabbed on to veruccas, warts and on other skin complaints (not near the eyes). It has strong anti-septic properties. Apply to veruccas daily until the wart is encapsu-lated and drops off. Available from The Turkish Oregano Company (www.originaumoil.com).

Peppermint An infusion made with mint is delicious and calming and helps to ease nausea and stomach upset.

Plantago A remedy for catarrh, glue ear and sinusitis. It combines well with Echinacea. Available from Bioforce (01294 277 344 or www.bioforce.co.uk).

Propolis Propolis (sometimes described as bee glue) tincture has anaesthetic as well as antibacterial properties and can be applied directly to a bite or sting. Available from Comvista (www.comvista.com).

Tea Tree Oil This is a highly effective antibacterial treatment, and can stop an infection setting in. Applied on a cotton bud, it can be used to gently swab out the outer ear canal to stop ear infections in their track. Head lice loathe tea tree and regular use of hair products containing tea tree oil will discourage them.

Slippery Elm This is the classic herb for helping to relieve stomach cramps, diarrhoea and constipation. Make a tea infusion and drink three or four times a day.

Steam A bowl of steaming boiled water with a towel placed over the head to form a tent is the best way to relieve congestion and phlegm. Inhale the steam for 5 minutes. You can add decongestant herbs such as Olbas Oil (eucalyptus, clove, menthol and other herbs) available from chemists. Obviously, take great care not to burn with hot water.

Toothpaste A little dab of toothpaste on a bite or sting neutralises it.

Zinc Lozenges For sore throats. Zinc has been shown to reduce the effects of viral infections. Ideally combine with Echinacea. Other good combinations include vitamin C, manuka honey and ginger.

Nature's Plus Kids' Zinc lozenges, available from health food shops, or Echinacea lozenges from Bioforce (01294 277 344 or www.bioforce.co.uk).

Immune Boost

Promoting the health of your child's immune system is one of the most important ways you can make sure your child is healthy and able to enjoy an active and energetic life. You can think of the immune system as an army that protects your child's body from assaults from the outside world. The various components of the immune system constantly patrol the blood and lymph system looking out for 'foes' – identifying them, tagging them, calling in reinforcements to do battle, defeating them and then finally clearing the debris away.

The Immune System is Responsible for Dealing With

- Viruses
- Bacteria
- Parasites
- Clearing away debris from cuts
- Allergy-causing substances
- Some toxins and chemicals

Prime Importance

A child is born with little of his own immunity, and this is one reason why breast feeding is important, as a mother's milk confers many immune factors to protect the child. Breast milk provides maternal antibodies (immune compounds) to get the baby through the first few months. Breast milk also helps the baby's digestive tract to mature, and this is an important barrier for immune self-defence against foreign bodies. As your child grows his own immune system is systematically 'primed', in its own right and over time, by being exposed to viruses.

It seems to many parents that their child has a permanently streaming nose, frequently runs a temperature and catches every bug going. This often starts in earnest at the point when the child is put with a childminder, or first attends a nursery or playgroup and is coming into more frequent contact with other children. This can be particularly worrying for first-time parents, who do not realise that it is perfectly normal for a child to build his immunity by catching all these bugs. By the time a child is about five years old this usually settles down and there are far fewer periods of illness. However, it is important to always keep an eye out for how any illness develops as some more serious ailments can, initially, mirror more common illnesses, such as the flu. Temperatures can rise and fall with alarming speed and illnesses develop rapidly in small children. If in doubt, always check with your doctor.

When the immune system comes into contact with a new virus, it is primed to respond and should therefore confer immunity against further attacks. However, some viruses are clever and have the ability to mutate into different strains – this is why something like the flu can be caught many times. Immunity is not acquired to bacterial infections or parasite infestations, but a healthy immune system will deal with them most effectively.

Allergies are a different kind of immune reaction where the response is an excessive one to a substance that does not cause an immune reaction in other people. Allergy problems, such as asthma and hay fever, are on the increase and by supporting immune health it has been demonstrated that children have greater resistance to immune challenges such as allergic reactions.

Diet and Immunity

Some babies seem to be more robust than others from the word go, and we all have a genetic blueprint that means that some children will have stronger, or weaker, immune systems than the norm. However this genetic programming is only a part of the story, and how we nurture our child's health will make a huge difference in how the immune system actually performs when faced with illnesses and other challenges.

Another reason to take a keen interest in your child's immune health is that there are links between good physical health and learning and development. Nutrients, such as iron, zinc and vitamin C, which are needed for a healthy immune system, are also important for mental function, growth and energy production.

Diet can also serve to undermine your child's immune system. One of the chief culprits is too much sugar. While sugar provides calories it is devoid of any nutrients, which means that an excess acts as a 'stressor' on the immune system. For children, the main sources are likely to be too many cordials, excessive juices away from meals (some with meals is fine), and too many sweets. Another potential problem is if your child is allergic, or just intolerant, to foods. The main culprit is often milk (and other dairy products). If your child has persistent immune problems, such as excessive mucus (more than his friends have), glue ear, eczema and asthma, you might find it useful to experiment with a trial period of dairy avoidance to see if this makes a difference. If you establish that this is an issue then you will need to make sure that your child does not miss out nutritionally in the long run. *See* Milk and Dairy, page 162.

Immune Boosters

The point about this list is that the more colourful your child's plate of food is, the more good it will do.

	Rich in	*Good for*
Apples	Quercetin	Antioxidant useful for lungs.
	Pectin	A fibre which helps to detoxify pollution.
Bananas	Potassium	Brain function, nerve cells and water balance.
Berries	Proanthocyanidins	The dark red colouration supports immune health. Especially good for lungs and heart health.
Broccoli/	Glucosinolates	Anti-cancer compound.
Cabbage	Indole-3-carbinol	Anti-cancer compound.
Cantaloupe/ Carrot	Beta-carotene	Eye, skin and lung health.
Citrus	Vitamin C	Antioxidant, used for energy production, needed for immune health, and to make collagen (necessary for skin and bone health).
	Bioflavonoids	Makes vitamin C more potent.
	Limonene	Helps liver to function.
Cherries	Proanthocyanidins	See berries above.
	Iron	Builds blood.

Garlic/ Onion	Aliin/alicin	Boosts white blood cells.
Ginger	Gingerol	Antioxidant.
Grapes	Ellagic acid	Antioxidant.
	Magnesium	Nerve function and bowel health.
Mango	Beta-carotene	See cantaloupe above.
	Galic acid	Good for bowel health.
Mushrooms (Oriental)	Polysaccharides	Immune/white blood cell stimulants.
Papaya	Papain	Enzyme that aids digestion
	Vitamins A, C & E	The three main antioxidant vitamins.
Pineapple	Bromelain	Enzyme that aids digestion.
Tomatoes	Lycopene	Antioxidant.
Watermelon	Potassium	See bananas above.
	Lycopene	Potent antioxidant protective against some cancers.

Reducing the Load

The following can help to improve the situation for those with hay fever, asthma, migraines or eczema (*see also* relevant sections under Food as Medicine, page 71). They are more likely to work together as a multi-pronged approach, but will have no effect against serious allergic reactions, such as to peanuts or bee stings.

- Evaluating food sensitivities – While these are different to allergies, they are still relevant. Food sensitivities have the effect of putting a stress on the body and this, in turn, makes a susceptible child more vulnerable to allergic reactions. Common sensitivities that exacerbate allergies include wheat, soya and dairy. For more on these *see* Food Intolerances, page 82.

- Oily fish or fish oil supplements – The fatty acids contained in oily fish, such as mackerel, sardines, tuna and salmon, are potent tools in the fight against all allergies, but particularly asthma, as they help to reduce inflammation. Two or three portions a week, or daily fish oil supplements, can make a huge difference.

- Fruit and vegetables – These are packed with antioxidants. Since all allergy reactions involve free radicals generated from inflammation these are vital to protect delicate body tissues. Children who eat more fruit and veg are less susceptible to allergies.

- A child-formulated vitamin and mineral supplement – This is really just for insurance. There are many nutrients involved in bolstering the immune system and because children can be erratic eaters and are growing fast, which makes a call on their reserves, a supplement as a part of a comprehensive approach will help. *See* X-tra Insurance – Supplements, page 274.

- Cutting out excess sugar and sugary drinks – Excess sugar directly affects the immune system in a negative way. It is a stress on the body and reduces the ability to produce certain white blood cells. A little won't hurt, but if your child is binging on sugar it certainly won't help. *See* Sugar, page 224.

- Cutting out food colourings – These are particularly implicated in asthma and eczema. Keeping your child off bright, artificial food colourings found in drinks, sweets, cordials and jellies is an important step. *See* Labels II – Additives, page 134.

The Great Outdoors

Physical activity is an important primer of the immune system. Unfortunately, some children can spend as many as 22 hours indoors, and the electronic nanny (TV) is a tempting way for parents to get a little peace and quiet. This means that children are nowhere near as active as they once where. Fresh air may also be important in another way. While we think of pollution as being an outdoor problem (car exhaust, farming chemicals, etc) in fact pollution levels, from chemicals used routinely around the house, are several times higher indoors. What was once achieved with soap and a scrubbing brush, now takes several different anti-bacterial sprays to accomplish. The very germs we are trying to get rid of may well be useful for priming the young immune system, and the chemicals used in household aerosols, sprays and powders may well help to also suppress our immune systems. This could have a serious impact on children and could be a part of the reason why we are seeing increases in allergy problems such as asthma, hay fever and eczema. Certainly asthma remains rare in countries where outside life is the norm.

One of the current debates is whether grubby children are actually a good thing. It seems that those who wash less frequently, and whose homes are less than pristine, are actually less likely to suffer from problems such as asthma as their immune systems may have been primed in early childhood. It also seems that a cat in the house from early babyhood is likely to mean a lower risk of developing a cat allergy, again as the immune system is primed early on. This whole area of investigation is fairly new at the moment, but is offering some interesting clues.

Vitamins, Herbs, Tonics and Tinctures

By far the most important immune boosting measure is to ensure your child eats five portions of fruits and vegetables (size adjusted for how small your child is, *see* page 88).

- As children can be erratic eaters it will do no harm to give your baby child-formulated vitamin drops from the age of six months (follow the dosage instructions).
- Cod liver oil was always given to children during the winter

months in past decades to good effect. Nowadays, I prefer to give fish oils, which come from muscle meat, because the liver of the fish (as in cod or halibut liver oil) is more likely to be contaminated.

- Encourage a taste for garlic and use it liberally in your food. Garlic is one of the most ancient and effective immune supporters.

- A daily teaspoonful of Sambucol (www.naturesstore.co.uk) is an excellent preventive step against colds and sniffles, and other respiratory tract infections.

- Immune boosting herbs such as echinacea and cat's claw can be useful in the winter months, but should only be given to children with advice from a qualified herbalist about dosages when using the whole herbs. You can now safely buy echinacea products specifically designed for kids. Holland and Barrett Echinacea for Kids (www.hollandandbarrett.com) or Echinacea for Kids Farmacia (0870 111 8123).

- Immune system boosters also include having fun, laughter, getting enough sleep and exercise

Old Wives' Tales

An apple a day keeps the doctor away
TRUE: Apples, along with other fruit, are valuable sources of antioxidants which are vital for immune health. In particular, apples support lung health.
Rub a gold ring/penny on a stye and it will go away
FALSE: This will make no difference. Styes are more likely when the immune system is run down.

Feed a cold, starve a fever

TRUE: If a child has a fever it is unlikely that he will be hungry, so keep meals light, but keep fluid levels up to avoid dehydration. Colds rarely interfere with hunger.

Vinegar on the chest will cure a cold

FALSE: Vinegar or rubs on the chest may help to 'open' the breathing passages, but will not directly affect the viruses responsible for colds.

Garlic keeps vampires and flu at bay

TRUE: Not sure about vampires, but garlic is certainly a potent antiviral agent (as well as being antibacterial and antifungal). Regularly including garlic in the diet keeps children healthy.

Freezing or burning off a verrucca is the only way to get rid of it

FALSE: This is painful and unnecessary. A strong immune system will ensure they are 'encapsulated' and simply drop off eventually.

Junk Food

We are seeing a whole generation of children grow up to be junk food junkies. This habit is firmly established in childhood, though parents often do not see that their child is really affected. It is easy to think that giving in to crisps or sodas is OK because, say, your child does not have a weight problem and so it really doesn't matter what he eats, or he's growing just fine, or it's better to eat something rather than nothing. But occasional habits become frequent ones and before you know it you have a teenager on your hands who will eat nothing but junk and you are throwing your hands up in despair. Of course it doesn't mean that you need to be such a purist that your child never has even one taste of junk or fast food – this is also probably not practical given that they will be going to birthday parties and visiting other people's houses. But if you find that these foods dominate, your child is likely to be losing out in the health stakes.

Children need concentrated sources of nutrients to fuel the growing they have to do. And it is not just growth, but healthy growth that is at stake. Children are getting taller (and wider!) because they are getting more than enough calories for this growth. But they are not getting healthier, because, while junk foods provide plenty of calories, these calories are depleted of the nutrients needed for basic good health. Junk food habits are contributing to a number of health problems in children:

- Tiredness, listlessness and lack of energy
- Lack of enthusiasm about physical activity
- Mood swings, irritability or restlessness
- Unpredictable behaviour
- Constipation or loose bowels
- Weight problems
- Pale skin, dull hair, dark shadows under eyes
- Tummy aches, nausea, headaches
- Frequent colds, infections or other illnesses
- Poor concentration

It is commonly said by nutritionists that there is no such thing as a bad food, just a bad diet. What they mean is that any food can be incorporated into a diet as long as it is in the right proportion. A little sweetie won't do any harm if the main diet is focussed on healthy foods. But any parent who has been faced with a child attempting to eat a whole packet of jelly-filled, sugar-coated marshmallows washed down with a cola, knows that there is such a thing as really bad food. The problem is that these foods, and similar, are:

1) The thin end of the wedge and children can and do, when left to their own devices, easily fill up on these all the time.
2) Advertised in such a way that nutritious foods barely get a look in. They are often promoted as 'XX per cent fat free' or 'with added vitamins' and so on, which is enough to confuse any person.

With a young child you have the advantage of a blank sheet and you can educate that child's palate, habits and mind set. Even as they grow older and more independent, by establishing a taste for real food early on you have done valuable 'programming' which can be relied upon to create a healthy framework, even if they stray from time to time, or for whole chunks of time, later on.

If you have only recently overhauled the family's eating habits, however, and older children are being 're-educated', you may have more of a struggle on you hands. The trick is not to give up and to be consistent in your approach. If you keep going, eventually you will make a difference. You will just need to go slowly and keep praising any positive changes that are made.

So What Can You Do?

Stock the House with Real Food If there are no packets of junky snacks around then the choice to eat them is not there. Instead fill your larder with enticing wholefood options. *See* Munchies, page 169, for ideas.

Do Not Force New Foods Encourage and praise. When a new food is accepted reward with a compliment. Many exposures might be needed to achieve acceptance. Research tells us that it can take up to ten exposures to a food for it to be accepted, but parents usually give up after two or three attempts. If the food is rejected, simply remark that perhaps next time it will be enjoyed. Find interesting ways to introduce the food.

Be a Role Model There is no point in asking your child to do what you do not. Without pressure simply eat a nutritious diet as a family and your child will, eventually, follow suit. Be prepared to experiment with new foods and tastes yourself.

Junk Food Tastes When you are developing your child's taste buds away from the homogeneity of junk food you are rejecting bland foods in favour of fresh tastes, you are replacing pulpy textures with real textures, and moving away from depending on salty, fatty foods towards tastes with 'life' in them. In other words towards real food. Spell out, whenever you can, what you think about Ugggghh foods. Keep repeating the mantras without being 'preachy', but just pointing out how it is for you when you taste it. Remark on how salty a snack is and how it makes you thirsty, or how something is so sweet that it is cloying and sickly, or how another food is like eating a greaseball, or the fatty taste is sticking to the roof of your mouth, or even if something tastes chemically. Do the opposite with real foods and comment, for instance, on how the strawberries have a sweet and sharp taste, the fish has a delicate taste, the subtle blend of spices in another dish give it a delicious aroma and taste.

Instant Gratification One of the easiest ways for your children to fall back on junk food habits is to satisfy urges for instant filling and strong-tasting food. The only way to beat this is to always have really delicious quick snacks and meals readily to hand that are also nutritious. You will find plenty of suggestions throughout the book, and in the various serving suggestions. These are some of the choices you will be teaching your child to make:

21st Century Pap		For real	
Cloying and artifically sweetened	Sugary cereals, sugary children's yoghurt and desserts, jelly, colas, 'juice' drinks.	Naturally sweet	Bananas, raisins, fruit, mild yoghurts
Refined	White bread, white rice, chips	Whole-foods	Wholemeal breads, brown rice, porridge oats, home-made popcorn, baked potatoes, nuts, seeds, crackers (oatcakes, rye)
Pulpy textures	Yoghurts with 'no bits', ready-made mousses and desserts	Real textures	Fresh fruit, meals with a variety of crunchy textures (e.g. stir-fries)
Boring	Repetitious, heavily salted flavours, lacking in variety, manufactured foods	Colourful	The rainbow colours of fresh fruits and vegetables

Kids in the Kitchen

Involving children in cooking is great fun. There is no need to rely on the latest pre-packaged cartoon character tea-cake mixture. Just look in your larder for inspiration and you are away. Children get a real sense of achievement when they turn out something edible. They also love to make gifts for people and you can stock up on little boxes, paper plates and tissue paper to gift-wrap their offerings.

Baking is the easiest for children to get into, but any aspect of cooking will inspire them. Children usually want fairly instant results, and dishes like pancakes are ideal, but as they get older and more practised dishes that take longer, like a stew, become more likely. There are many cookery books aimed at children which you can find in your library. Experimenting with these basic recipes is also a fast track to learning about weights and measures in a more practical way than any maths class. The rudiments of kitchen hygiene and food safety are also absorbed without effort.

Do your best not to lose your cool, as cooking with children can be quite messy, and clearing up may not be as interesting to them as chopping, peeling and cooking. But the advantage is that you are entertaining your child for a while, without resorting to the TV, and teaching a valuable skill for life (and he won't even know about the last bit!). Safety is always important and extra care must be taken with hot ovens, kettles, boiling liquids, hot pan handles, knives and other sharp instruments.

The final test of your commitment to encouraging your child to cook, when he is a little older, is to encourage him to make the family a meal once a week. You will need courage, the willingness to watch your kitchen descend into chaos and the fortitude to keep out unless asked for advice (and possibly an iron stomach to eat the results), but the confidence that comes from this exercise is immeasurable. It does not have to be an elaborate meal and a bowl of pasta or some eggs on toast are easily within the reach of most young cooks.

Ideas for Kids in the Kitchen

- At the most simple level building a fun sandwich is a favourite. Different breads – bagels, croissants, pitta pockets or rye – can be used with a number of fillings. Melted sandwiches are more adventurous: try tuna, avocado and mozzarella cheese (melted under the grill) or baked banana and chocolate.
- Chopped salad ingredients with something moist, such as salad dressing, mayonnaise, cream cheese or hummus, and some protein, such as chopped ham or egg, wrapped up in a tortilla is a great way to use up leftovers.
- Pizzas are a favourite. Make the dough in a bread machine and and top with tomato sauce and chopped vegetables. Have a competition for who can design the funniest face out of vegetables.
- If you have a bread machine then all sorts of recipes become

easy for a child – peanut butter bread, ginger loaf, banana and walnut bread, teabread. Of course, you don't have to have a bread machine and it is fun to knead the dough and let it rise, but a machine is a good half-way house between creativity and fairly instant gratification.

- Anything in a blender or food processor is fun (teaching safety first). Children love to make a noise and add ingredients. They can make soups, sauces, smoothies, ice cream sodas, fools and puddings. Soups are also a good way to deal with a glut of seasonal vegetables, and smoothies use up inexpensive summer fruits.
- Avocado halves filled with prawns in dressing, with chopped mango or with dressed chopped tomatoes are easy, delicious and look attractive.
- Tacos can be filled with any number of things – sliced avocado or guacamole dip, yoghurt, re-fried beans, cooked minced meat, chopped tomato, grated cheese.
- A pretty fruit plate can bring out the artist in your child.
- Children love to make popcorn.
- Make cheese straws in the shape of noughts and crosses and have a game before you eat them.
- Make a basic bread recipe to the dough stage. Divide the dough into two equal amounts and press one lot into the loaf tin. Before placing the second half on top put several cubes of high quality chocolate in between. Seal the top half down. Bake as usual and when the bread is cut lots of gooey chocolate spills out from the middle.
- Anything that can be threaded on a barbecue stick and grilled is a favourite. Chunks of fish, cherry tomatoes, onion quarters, pineapple pieces, ham cubes or marinated tofu are all good options (*see* Outdoor Eating, page 187, for marinade ideas).
- Beating eggs is always good news and the obvious next step is an omelette with a variety of filling choices. A Spanish omelette is easiest to make as it has a firm texture – add chopped, fried onion, red pepper and diced potato.

- Pasta in all its guises is easy and satisfying for children to make. If they are feeling a little more adventurous make stuffed pasta shapes from pasta sheets with your favourite filling – ricotta and spinach, for instance.

- Any rolling and stuffing is fun for a child, if a little messy. Stuffed vine leaves or rice and nut-stuffed baked peppers, falafel, meatballs and fish cakes are all good ideas.

- Grated salads are also a winner, just watch out for grated fingers. Carrot, cabbage and beetroot make a rainbow salad. Grated cheese can be added to all sorts of things. Grated raw potato can be added to finely chopped onion and fried into patties – potato latkas – or add finely chopped bacon and fry into rösti.

- Chunky-chip dippers are fun. Make baked potato wedgies and, when cool enough to handle, dip them in guacomole, salsa or aubergine dip.

- The simplest things are delicious – like fruit dipped in melted chocolate. Find something that small fingers find easy to handle, such as strawberries, starfruit, physyllis or grapes.

- Pancake batter can be whizzed in the blender in seconds and when cooked can be filled with sweet or savoury fillings. Savoury: mushroom, chopped spring onion and red pepper, ham and mozzarella, asparagus and cheese. Sweet: lemon and sugar, banana and raisin, Greek yoghurt and honey.

- A stir-fry with spring onions, sliced mushrooms, prawns and rice – or anything else you have to hand, such as shredded cooked chicken, sweetcorn and red pepper slivers – is always popular.

- Good presents for children to make, apart from cakes, muffins and biscuits, are relishes, bottled fruit, herby salad dressings in attractive bottles, and dried fruit.

Kitchen Hygiene

When teaching children about food and cooking, you also need to get them into good kitchen hygiene habits. While there is a good theory that a few bugs are beneficial for us, helping to build up our immune systems, the kitchen is a trouble spot for food poisoning bugs such as salmonella. Get your child into good habits early and the risks are reduced.

Basic Rules

- Always wash hands, with soap, after going to the toilet.
- Always wash hands, with soap, before handling food.
- Do not handle pets and food at the same time, wash your hands with soap.
- When you get back from shopping store perishable foods at once. A chicken in the back of a hot car for half an hour becomes an extraordinary breeding ground for bacteria.
- Keep raw meat on the lowest shelf of your refrigerator with cooked meats on higher shelves. This avoids blood dripping on to, and contaminating, cooked foods, which will not subsequently be heated to sufficiently high temperatures to kill any bacteria.
- Cook foods thoroughly to kill bacteria. Meat juices should run clear when tested with a skewer.
- Barbecues are a particular risk as food is often cooked on the outside but raw or rare inside.
- Get in to the habit of checking the 'sell-by' and 'use-by' dates on packs. Sell-by means there is still a day or two leeway before something needs to be thrown out. Use-by is a final date by which the food can be eaten.

- Sell-by and use-by dates assume that food is stored according to instructions. If this is not the case, the dates may no longer apply.
- Always follow the manufacturer's instructions regarding freezing and defrosting.
- Do not use chopping boards, knives, kitchen towels, etc. for raw meats and then re-use on vegetables or bread which will be eaten without cooking.
- Scrub chopping boards thoroughly when washing them and allow to air-dry.
- When handling raw meat be aware that food poisoning bacteria is often spread by touch – by taps or cupboard handles touched before washing hands – so lever taps that can be turned on with your elbow are ideal.

Kitchen Shortcuts

Most people do not have the time or inclination to spend hours in the kitchen. It helps, therefore, to have some short-cuts readily to hand when faced with a hungry hoard. Here are some ideas:

- When roasting or baking double up the use of the oven by putting in other things. Roast vegetables in a pan alongside a roast joint and they will all be done at the same time (add the veg half-way through). Slip some potatoes in to bake and 20–30 minutes before they are done bake some fish in tomato, herbs and olive oil.
- Steaming is a healthy way to cook and is fast. You can layer two or three baskets on top of each other. The advantage of steaming is that it preserves nutrients and brings out the flavour of the food. Afterwards, if you wish, you can toss vegetables in a little lemon juice, balsamic vinegar, sesame oil or olive oil. Steaming

is ideal for the delicate flavour of fish.

- Get into the habit of making double quantities of anything that might possibly freeze well, such as stews, chilli, Bolognese, soups, casseroles.

- Keep ingredients that can be thrown together into tasty salads or used to bulk out a shop-bought fresh soup and turn it into a meal readily to hand. Cans of beans (cannellini, kidney, flageolet, chickpeas), chopped red peppers, tuna, sliced mushrooms and pasta shapes are all good for this.

- Children love a plate of pick-'n'-mix. Arrange in an attractive way four or five of the following: sticks of cheese, a dollop of hummus, rolled up ham strips, breadsticks, wholewheat crackers, pitta fingers, cucumber slices, carrot sticks, pitted olives, a few grapes, tangerine segments, apple slices.

- Stock cubes never taste as good as home-made stock. Save meat bones and chicken carcasses in the freezer for a few weeks until you are ready to make stock. Cover with water and bring to the boil. Add scrubbed root vegetables, onions and garlic and simmer for at least a couple of hours. Strain off the stock, cool, skim off the fat, and freeze in portion sizes. Using real stock for your risottos, soups and stews will make them taste fabulous and as the stock is rich in minerals from the bones and vegetables it will be extra-healthy for your family.

Labels I – Deciphering Them

It used to be said that, given the regulations about precise listings of fibre contents, a consumer could find out more about the ingredients in their socks, than they could about the food they were eating. It's got a little better, but things are still not particularly clear and consumers remain totally confused.

Nutrition Panels

These are not compulsory but most products carry them. A quick look will tell you if a product fits within healthy-eating guidelines. We all know that, ideally, we should eat a little, and not a lot of, sugar or salt, for instance, but what exactly do these terms mean?

These figures are per 100 g of product or per complete packaged meal portion.

	THIS IS A LOT	THIS IS A LITTLE
SUGAR	10 g	2 g
SODIUM (SALT)	0.5 g (1.25 g)	0.1 g (0.25 g)
TOTAL FAT	20 g	3 g
SATURATED FAT	5 g	1 g

Source: Food Standards Agency, London.

Ingredient Listing

In order to clear up much confusion with food product labelling, QUIDs was introduced quite recently. QUIDs stands for quantative ingredient declarations. It spells out the following rules:

- The quantity of an ingredient must be declared as a percentage of the total if it appears in the name of the food (for example, broccoli and cheese pie must declare how much broccoli and how much cheese) or if the ingredient is usually associated with the dish (for example, the vegetables as a percentage of a spring roll).
- The amounts also have to be stated if the ingredient or image features on the pack (for example, 'made with cream' or a photo of strawberries on a yoghurt).
- The exceptions to the above are:

  - if the ingredient is in tiny quantities as a flavouring
  - the product consists of a single ingredient

- the product has a 'customary name', such as peanut butter, which does not contain butter
- the amounts are obvious from the drained weight stated on canned goods (for example, 425 g beans)
- it is an unlabelled product, or in small packs, or is a mixture with no predominant ingredient (say Bombay mix, sold loose)
- the ingredient is not likely to influence the choice of the buyer (for example, soya in soya infant formula or sesame seeds on sesame seed buns)

As a result of the above you should be able to easily identify if a product has a significant amount of what is stated in the name of the product, but it is only by using a bit of mental arithmetic that you can work out the quantities of what else might be in the product. So, for example, if the label on the broccoli and cheese pie says it is 20 per cent pastry, 10 per cent cheese, 7 per cent broccoli (totalling 37 per cent), you have to ask yourself what makes up the remaining 63 per cent. Ingredients such as starch and milk may be listed, but without any amount, so the balance is likely to be these, plus a large amount of water, (which does not have to be declared unless it exceeds 10 per cent of the weight of meat, although up to 30 per cent of a meat product can be water). The starch and the water would be referred to by nutritionists as 'low-nutrient fillers', because they are ingredients that do not confer any nutritious advantages. Additionally, because the majority of the product (the starch and water) is tasteless paste, you can guarantee that a quick check of the sodium listing will reveal that the product is high in salt in order to add some flavour.

QUIDs is far from perfect – there are far too many exceptions to the rule, plus rules that can be bent or simply ignored by the food manufacturers because the penalties are paltry. As a result, many companies do not give straightforward ingredient listings that can be understood by people without a degree in food technology.

The 25 per cent rule

One issue that parents need to be aware of, especially if their children have allergies, is the 25 per cent rule. At the moment, any composite ingredient which makes up less than 25 per cent of the total product does not have to have its ingredients listed. In other words, salami on a pizza can just be described as salami, rather than divided into its individual ingredients of beef, pork, milk powder, starch, spices, etc. The problem with this is that ingredients to which a person might be allergic are not highlighted. There is a good chance, however, that this exception will be abolished by 2005.

Flavourings

Added flavours and flavourings do not have E-numbers. There are in excess of 3,000 permitted chemical flavourings and they can be listed simply as flavouring on ingredient listings. The terminology is confusing, and it really is an exercise in semantics:

Natural Flavour Derived from natural food sources.

Natural Flavouring Same chemical formula as the natural ingredient but manufactured in a laboratory and made from petrochemicals. They are more durable, and cheaper, and so are favoured by food manufacturers.

Flavouring Artificial flavours. They usually make up for lack of flavours in products which use low-nutrient fillers and water to bulk them out. Often means monosodium glutamate (MSG).

What to Spot on the Pot

- Don't be taken in by healthy looking fruit on the package. A good example is raspberry flavoured yoghurt. 'Flavoured' means artificial flavouring, but if it said 'Flavour' the flavour would have to come from real raspberries. Confused?
- Colourings which are natural and not harmful include beetroot red, beta-carotene, curcumin, riboflavin, leutein, xanthine and anthocyanins.
- Fillers, stabilisers and gums allow for more use of cheap ingredients such as water. They are not intrinsically harmful but the presence of these low-nutrient additives means that 'real food' is not being used.
- Hydrogenated vegetable oil is common in the food manufacturing industry but has been criticised by many nutritionists for being implicated in childhood asthma, eczema and other allergic conditions. Maximum levels are now being made compulsory.
- The cheekiest type of claim on many products is 'with added vitamins' or 'a good source of vitamin X'. These products with added nutrients, often sugary cereals, sweets or sugary 'juice' drinks, are enticing parents with the claim to make them feel better about giving their child the food in question. But adding vitamins to a sweet does not magically make an unhealthy product healthy. It still remains loaded with sugar and fats.
- It also seems that no product is complete without a 'Parents' Checklist' on the side, such as on this yoghurt carton:

No fruit bits
Made with real fruit purée
Natural colour
Suitable for vegetarians
Gluten free

Of course these lists pander to our desire to do something right for the health of our children, without really saying very much at all: you would expect a yoghurt to be gluten free and suitable for vegetarians anyway! Often it is not what they say on the checklist that is important, but what they don't say. Beware of omissions. If 'No preservatives' and 'No artificial sweeteners' are listed that is terrific, but why don't they also scream 'No artificial colour'? A look at the full ingredient list will tell you why when you spot the inclusion of E124 (which is Ponceau 4R, a red colouring).

Health and Other Claims

There are a number of flashes, marketing terms and claims which are mostly fairly confusing and often meaningless. Additionally, pictures are often used to convey a feeling of health and freshness, such as a picture of fruit on the front of a package.

Terms such as 'Fresh' are meaningless, as in fresh pasta in a canned ravioli with an expiry date two years hence. 'Country style', 'Farmhouse' and 'Authentic' are all equally meaningless. 'Pure', along with 'Natural', are not defined in law and do not always mean what you think they do.

'Lite' and 'Light', 'Low-Fat' and 'Fat-Free' should not, to quote the Food Standards Agency website, 'be taken at face value'. A reduced-fat food can still be fairly high in calories or with lots of added sugar. For instance, crisps are a high-fat food and even their reduced-fat counterparts will be high in fat. If a product has a flash across it saying it is 95 per cent fat-free the remaining 5 per cent (which is fat) can easily make up 30 per cent of the calories. There is nothing wrong with 30 per cent calories from fat (and is in fact within government healthy-eating guidelines) but the 95 per cent fat-free is designed to confuse as it sounds a lot better than 30 per cent calories from fat. If you are wondering how this works, each gram of fat is 9 calories. So 5 g of fat (what is left after the 95 per cent that is not fat) is 45 calories. You will find that 45 calories as a percentage of the calories from the full 100 g of product will be somewhere between 25–35 per cent depending on the product.

'Reduced Salt' or 'Reduced Sodium' means that a product is lower than its same 'full-salt' product but it does not mean it is actually a low-salt product and the amounts may still be high.

Quality Assurance marks are often used to convey an idea that products conform to certain standards, but these are voluntary schemes which are not always aimed at consumer benefit but at promoting particular groups of manufacturers. Lion mark eggs are, however, virtually guaranteed to be free of salmonella – you can get both organic and non-organic lion mark eggs.

See also Labels II – Additives, page 134, Sweeteners, page 228, and Organic Eating, page 187, for a description of organic labelling.

Labels II – Additives

According to a recent report from The Food Commission, 38 per cent of children's foods contain additives, and this figure excluded soft drinks, sweets, chocolate and crisps. This chemical burden being placed on our children, along with the chemical burden of pesticides, is a source of concern for many parents.

But food additives in processed foods are also the source of much confusion for parents. There is a general feeling that all additives are a bad thing, particularly when they are expressed as E-numbers, but this is not necessarily the case. Not all E-numbers are bad. For example, some are natural antioxidants, such as vitamin C, natural colourings such as beetroot, or thickeners such as pectin. E-numbers are quoted less on labels these days (rather than the actual name of the additive) as they just tend to scare people.

On the other hand, there are many suspect additives used, in particular artificial food colourings and preservatives. Symptoms in children which have been attributed to consuming these, whether there is a known sensitivity or not, include behavioural problems, asthma and urticaria (nettle rash). A recent government-funded study by the UK's Asthma & Allergy Research Centre found behaviour changes, including educational difficulties, in three-year-old children consuming artificial colourings and sodium benzoate preservative, even if they did not have a history of hyperactivity or allergic reactions. In the period when they were given the additives in a drink there was an increase in disturbing others, difficulty getting to sleep, poor concentration and temper tantrums. When the additives were removed there were marked beneficial changes in behaviour.

One way to avoid synthetic additives is to make sure that any prepared foods you buy are organic. Around 66 additives are permitted in organic food production but these must be from natural sources and exclude sweeteners and colourings. Organic food allows flavours to be added. *See* Organic Eating, page 181.

Preservatives

Adverse reactions, including asthma, have been linked to benzoates (E210–19), the antioxidants BHA and BHT (E320–21), and the sulphur preservatives (E220–8). While these are not always all that conducive to perfect health, some preservatives, such as the nitrates, are a necessity for some types of perishable foods which would be a risk to public health from bacterial contamination if the preservatives were not used. This can be easy to get round if you go for better quality fresh foods. You could also use frozen foods without preservatives instead of their chill-cabinet counterparts which have preservatives in them (though check the labels to make sure they are preservative free).

Colourings

Colourings are ubiquitous in children's foods, even if you put aside the obvious culprits such as drinks and sweets. Another report, from Organix Foods, found colourings in 14 per cent of dried fruit packs, 15 per cent of kid's frozen burgers, 32 per cent of crisps and savoury snacks, 24 per cent of kid's cheeses, 23 per cent of kid's cereals and 78 per cent of children's desserts.

It is a particular concern that many foods specifically targeted at children contain the worst of the food colourings (E102–80), including the azo dyes. For instance, jellies, mousse desserts, sodas, 'juice' drinks and sweets use artificial colours such as tartrazine (E102), quinoline yellow (E104), sunset yellow (E110), carmoisine (E122), ponceau 4R (E124) and green S (E142). Some children's medicines also use these colourings. The latest astounding idea is food colouring in sugar that kids paint directly on to their tongues to change tongue colour. Hopefully this product will go the same way as the flavoured vegetables, such as baked bean flavoured cauliflower, which sank without a trace.

Children with asthma, eczema, rhinitis and urticaria, or who are hyperactive, should definitely avoid food colourings, many of which have been banned elsewhere, such as in Scandinavian countries. Instead, choose products that use natural colourings, which are not harmful, such as beetroot red, beta-carotene, curcumin, riboflavin, leutein, xanthine and anthocyanins. They are more expensive for the food industry to use but are not detrimental to health.

Flavourings

Around 4,000 food additives are allowed in the UK, but not all can be found listed on labels. The reason is that there are more than 3,000 chemicals that can be listed simply as 'flavouring'. In order to avoid these, you need to choose foods which, for instance, contain 'strawberry flavour', which is derived from real strawberries, rather than 'strawberry flavour*ing*', which is synthetically derived. One flavour additive that is used extensively is MSG (Monosodium glutamate or E621), which is linked to bad reactions including headaches and 'Chinese Restaurant Syndrome' (which includes faintness and sweating). For more on MSG, *see* Salt Sellers, page 213.

Additives that are Likely to be Ok

It is not particularly useful, to list all the allowed additives as there are more than 900 of them. Of more use, is a list of those that are beneficial or benign. If the additive you are looking at does not appear below, you might at least be suspicious.

Colourings		Antioxidants	
E100	curcumin	E300–304	ascorbates (vitamin C)
E101	riboflavin		
E140	chlorophyll	E306–309	tocopherols (vitamin E)
E160	carotene		
E161	lutein and xanthins	Emulsifiers, stabilisers and others	
E162	beetroot		
E163	anthocyanins	E322	lecithins
E170	calcium carbonate (chalk)	E330–31	citrates
		E335–37	tartrates
E172	iron oxides	E350–53	malates
Preservatives		E353	metatartaric acid

E234	nisin	E355	adipic acid
E260	acetic acid	E363	succinic acid
E262	sodium diacetate	E375	nicotinic acid
E263	calcium acetate		(vitamin B3)
E290	carbon dioxide	E400–05	alginates
E297	fumaric acid	E406	agar-agar
E516	calcium sulphate	E440	pectin
E528	magnesium	E501	potassium
	hydrodoxide		carbonate
E551–2	silicas	E503	ammonium
E559	kaolin		carbonate
E576	sodium gluconate		
E577	potassium gluconate		
E578	calcium gluconate		
E901	beeswax		

To find out more about additives read *What The Label Doesn't Tell You* by Sue Dibb. Another good reference guide is *E for Additives* by Maurice Hanssen and Jill Marsden.

See also Sweeteners, page 228, and Labels I – Deciphering Them, page 128.

Learning About Food

Food education begins in the home. At best, school can influence and contribute to a child's overall attitude towards food, but the real foundation of the child's belief system will be laid at home. Making the whole process fun and exploratory, and weaving it into your daily life will give great rewards. Food education can help your child to become, ultimately, more self-sufficient and confident about feeding himself.

Food Families

Teaching your children about the basic food groups helps them to understand why it is important to eat well. Start by familiarising them with the basic food groups. Work with the groupings mentioned for making up lunchboxes on page 147 – protein foods (meat, fish, pulses, etc.), starches (potatoes, rice, bread), fruits and vegetables, calcium-rich foods (cheese, milk, yoghurt, canned sardines, sprats, kale, nuts and seeds). It is important to make it fun. Use real foods if you can, exploring smell, taste, texture. Use coloured crayons to draw and write. The following ideas are for children of a variety of ages, or can be adapted so they are more age-appropriate.

Food Games

- Cut out food pictures from magazines and play with them to build up pictures.
- Play guess the food. Put a blindfold on and then put out a tray of foods to either feel or taste. While you could use foods that might be a little challenging, such as pickles, remember not to spring any nasty surprises – trust is all. Get your child to guess the food and the group it belongs to. Now it's your turn!
- Take the above exercise into real life. Teach your child to enjoy the tastes and textures of real foods. Encourage them to learn to eat the crusts on bread, to crunch a few watermelon seeds instead of picking out every last one of them (try it yourself, they taste good and are incredibly rich in potassium), get them to eat chicken drumsticks and spareribs, and to eat the skin on fish if you have made it crispy.
- Ask your child to help you to make up a lunchbox that contains all the main food groups (*see* Lunchbox Planning, page 147).

- Ask your child to bring back the school lunch menu and see how it measures up against the guidelines on page 219. By doing this you can help to impress upon your child the importance of eating a portion of fruit or vegetables at school lunches (it might be on offer but do they eat it?).
- Ask them what their favourite foods are and discuss how they fit in to the groupings.
- Discuss different ways you can prepare particular foods. For instance, carrots can be raw or cooked (boiled, steamed or roasted). They can be grated and shredded into salads or stews, or puréed to a creamy texture in soups. Carrot sticks can be used to scoop up dips. This is the beginning of cookery lessons as well. If you think your child is up to it, get him to grate a carrot (mind out for grated fingers!) or cut them into rounds and then into star shapes.
- Plan party meals together with favourite foods that fit into the groupings (*see* Party Time, page 193).
- Look in the refrigerator or the pantry together and see which foods fit which categories. Introduce the idea of balance. Are the available foods balanced? *See* Balancing the Diet Books, page 13.
- Give a list of foods from different countries and work together to fit them into *country* groupings (for example, pasta from Italy, curry from India, baguette from France). Where do the foods fit in with the *food* groupings?
- Make up a true or false game to see how they score. Get them to think of some questions – the sillier the better because children love the absurd. Some ideas:

  – Spaghetti grows on trees. (FALSE)
  – Chocolate comes from beans. (TRUE)
  – Potatoes count as a vegetable. (Nutritionally speaking, FALSE)
  – Peanuts are beans and grow underground. (TRUE)
  – Cordial is a fruit drink. (FALSE)

- Bombay duck is fish. (TRUE)
- Rice is a fruit. (FALSE)

- Watch TV adverts together. See which types of foods are advertised and how often. Are healthy foods advertised more often than less-healthy foods? Or is it the other way round? *See* Advertising Whoppers, page 4.
- Use story-telling time to encourage your child to be more adventurous about food choices. For instance, a mermaid taking your child by the hand under the seas and treating him to a banquet of strange delights – seaweed, snails in garlic, shrimp and prawns that needed peeling, octopus and so on (this was one of my son's favourite stories).
- Children are not taught about the basics and often do not know, believe it or not, why there are pigs on farms (because we eat them) or that strawberries grow in fields (they often think they just come in punnets). Explaining the obvious is sometimes necessary.

Education and Familiarisation Really Works

A major study has found that fussy eaters increased their fruit intake from 4 per cent of children to 100 per cent and their vegetable intake from 1 per cent to 83 per cent by familiarising them with these foods. And the improvements remained six months later. The programme is as effective when fruit and vegetables are directly pitched against sweets, chocolates and crisps – so it doesn't have to be either/or initially. It is simply a matter of familiarising children with health-giving fruits and vegetables, and encouraging them to develop a taste for them. The study also found that a majority of children actually asked their parents to buy fruit and vegetables that were not usually on their shopping list, which might suggest that the parents' habits were a contributing factor to their children not eating as many of these foods as they could. For information on The Food Dudes, *see* Advertising Whoppers, page 4.

What Food is Good for What

Young children understand food on their own terms. It is pointless telling them it will help their immunity, protect them from heart disease or keep their bowels healthy. Instead link foods to influences they can relate to:

- Help you to have strong bones and grow taller.
- Give you energy to help you to run faster on the football pitch.
- Help you to see in the dark.
- Make your brain work better in school.
- (And for teenagers) help to keep your skin clear and healthy.

One report has concluded that the worst way to get children to eat up their vegetables (or other food) is to keep on at them that it is healthy for them. This is probably true at the point when the food is poised between plate and mouth, but is different to general background awareness of the effects of food on health.

See also Holiday Eating, page 99, and Projects and Activities, page 207.

Learning Difficulties

Learning difficulties affect around one in ten children, and boys are affected more often than girls. It is important to realise, however, that while it is convenient to attach 'labels' such as dyslexia, dyspraxia, ADD and hyperactivity to learning disorders for treatment purposes, in reality the various disorders represent a range, or a spectrum of disorders. Each disorder can be experienced along a scale from very mild to severe, and often also co-exist with other disorders to make a spectrum of disorders. Because of these inter-relationships, diagnosis and treatment needs to be sensitive to all the possible permutations. From a nutritional/brain chemistry point of view similar things are probably going on: either an underlying inability to convert essential fatty acids (EFAs) into HUFAs (highly unsaturated fatty acids); or not getting enough HUFAs in the diet. Signs of EFA deficiency include dry skin, dry hair, increased urination, increased thirst and poor concentration – symptoms that are also frequently found in children with learning disorders.

As a result of mis-diagnosis or misunderstanding of learning diffi-culties, children can often be affected by self-esteem problems which also need recognition and help. The irony of this is that they are often incredibly bright with high IQs but do not have the ability to communicate this and so get very frustrated.

How Can Nutrition Help?

It is becoming evident that diet can affect behaviour and thus also learning. There seems to be a straightforward relationship between certain nutritional elements affecting brain and nerve function, which in turn affects moods and behaviour. However, it also appears that some groups of people have a genetically reduced ability to absorb, process or metabolise certain nutrients, which leads to a similar set of results. These are some of the most important to think about:

Essential and Long Chain Fatty Acids

Essential fatty acids are, as the name implies, essential for normal health. They are the vitamins of the fat world and are found in seeds, nuts, grains, soya beans and their oils. The most important of these, in terms of learning difficulties, are those that are turned by the body into a group of fatty acids called LCPs/HUFAs. But some groups of people are unable to effectively convert essential fats into LCPs (long chain polyunsaturated fats). This means that, for them, LCPs also become 'essential' from the diet. The best dietary sources of these LCPs are oily fish, such as mackerel, sardines, fresh tuna or salmon, or from supplementation. Some shellfish also provide reasonable amounts of the LCP DHA. Dr Jacqueline Stordy, author of *The LCP Solution*, says that research is finding that those with ADHD, dyslexia and other learning difficulties exhibit signs of LCP deficiency. These are, most often, dry skin, poor hair condition and brittle nails, increased thirst and increased urination. Additionally, she says that if you look at their blood in a laboratory you can see that red blood cell membranes lack the right structures.

Minerals

Certain nutritional minerals are needed for normal brain and nervous development. Chief amongst these are iron, zinc and selenium. Signs of iron deficiency can include poor learning; signs of zinc deficiency can include emotional disturbance; selenium deficiency is implicated in mood imbalance. Foods rich in these nutrients include:

Iron Lean red meat, dark poultry meat. Uptake from plant sources of iron, such as oats, peas, raisins and rice, can be improved by consuming some orange juice, or other vitamin C-rich food, with meals.

Zinc Lean red meat, dark poultry meat, seeds, nuts, cheese, wholegrains, beans, lentils.

Selenium Brazil nuts (best source), rice, seafood, wholegrains.

If a mineral deficiency exists, a course of supplements can help to redress the imbalance. However, it is best to seek the advice of a nutritional therapist who specialises in paediatrics as it is difficult for a parent to judge how much of a mineral to give a child since it is calculated according to body weight and age.

E-Numbers There are a whole range of artificial additives that appear to affect those with ADD/ADHD – in particular, bright artificial colourings in sweets, jellies and other foods marketed explicitly at children. Many of these colourings are banned in other countries, including America and Scandinavian countries. *See* Labels II – Additives, page 134.

Lead According to the Department for Environment, Food and Rural Affairs (DEFRA), studies involving large groups of children have shown that lead interferes with brain development and so affects IQ. Lead has also been linked to behaviour and educational problems. Lead from air pollution has been reduced, but the majority of lead comes from water intake and diet and residual environmental pollution. Children absorb more than three times as much lead compared to adults, and an estimated one in ten children are affected by high levels. Sources of exposure to lead include buying produce from the roadside, children eating tiny amounts of old paint flakes and children licking fingers contaminated with house dust and soil. Including foods in the diet that are good sources of iron and calcium, such as lean meat, canned sardines and salmon (with the bones), eggs, raisins and other dried fruit, greens, milk, cheese, fruit, nuts, seeds, pulses and potatoes, helps to eliminated lead.

Simple Steps to Make Nutrition Work

Not all children will respond to specific nutritional changes. For instance, two-thirds of dyslexic children respond to essential fat supplementation in trials and it takes three months of supplementation to see a measurable improvement. This means that one-third won't respond, and it may well be that a combined nutritional approach is needed for some children who are resistant to one particular change. These are some practical ways parents can help their children nutritionally:

- Base the diet on freshly prepared whole foods – lean meat, poultry, fish, grains, beans, vegetables, fruit.
- Eat oily fish once or twice a week. (If your family are vegetarian then using flax oil daily, in salads for example, is an alternative, as it has oils from the same family, but it is fish oils which were used in the trials and the debate about the body's ability to convert the vegetables source of essential fatty acids into HUFAs remains.)
- Avoid excess amounts of hydrogenated fats (margarine, biscuits, pastries and crisps) and saturated fats (animal fats), which interfere with the proper metabolism of essential fats.
- Avoid highly processed foods and drinks, particularly those which are high in sugar or which use artificial food colourings.
- Search out manufactured food options, such as yoghurts, snack bars and cakes, which do not have artificial additives such as colourings.
- Some parents find that wheat and dairy intolerances affect their children and that avoiding foods to which their child is intolerant makes a real difference.
- Water intake is important for concentration. Send your child to school with a water bottle and ask the teacher to make sure he is permitted to drink from it.

- See if LCP supplements make a difference. Effalex are the supplements used in the research to which Dr Stordy refers. They consist mainly of fish oils, with evening primrose oil and vitamin E.
- Further reading: *The LCP Solution – Nutritional Treatment for ADHD, Dyslexia and Dyspraxia* by Jacqueline Stordy, Ph.D.
- The Hyperactive Children's Support Group (HACSG), 71 Whyke Lane, Chichester PO19 7PD. Send an SAE for information on non-drug treatment of ADD/ADHD and advice on how to eliminate sugar and additive-laden foods. Visit www.hacsg.org.uk
- The Dyslexia Research Trust can be contacted on www.dyslexic.org.uk

Lunchbox Planning

Healthy and interesting packed lunches are easy to provide as long as you do a little advanced planning. The planning is necessary because, let's face it, 7.30 am is not the best time for most of us to fix the ideal lunchbox.

The trick is to have a ready checklist of options, and to be ahead of the game by stocking up and cooking food which can double up for a lunchbox the next day, or which freezes well in portion sizes.

Studies have shown that children who eat both a good breakfast and a nutritionally-balanced lunch, have improved concentration and better behaviour. As three-quarters of all children now have a packed lunch at school, appealing with nutritionally-balanced options becomes ever more important.

Having the right kit helps: A sturdy box with compartments for different foods so they don't squash up against each other. A leak-proof drink flask and cheerful cutlery in different colours. Little pots with well sealed lids for portion sizes of salads or lucky-dip fruit or vegetables selections. A good quality wide-necked flask, with a cup, for tasty soups is also ideal. If you are providing a carton drink (milk-shake or juice, for instance) also provide a small plastic bottle of plain water as well. Buy an insulated bag and a couple of ice packs to keep the food fresh.

It is a useful exercise to make up a duplicate box a couple of times, and to keep it at home for a tasting, to see what the food is like by the time it is eaten – this helps to avoid soggy, lifeless, warm food that you wouldn't want to eat either!

Lunchbox Checklist

The ideal, nutritionally-balanced lunchbox will include foods from each of these main food groups:

- Bread/cereal (starches/carbohydrates)
- Fruit
- Vegetable
- Meat or meat alternative (proteins)
- Calcium-rich foods
- A drink, ideally a 500 ml bottle of water

Bread, Cereal or Starch Group

Breads and cereals are sources of carbohydrates, fibre, B-vitamins and minerals.

- Aim to use wholemeal bread for sandwiches. Pitta pockets are ideal, but use non-soggy fillings! Other ideas include soft tortillas, chapattis, bagels or savoury scones.
- Use leftover pasta, cous cous, or rice for a salad in a box with chopped up sausages, tomatoes and peas or black-eyed beans,

cooked onion and red peppers – or make up your own combinations.

- Mini pizzas, or pizza slices, with a variety of toppings.
- Crackers, oatcakes, breadsticks or crispbreads with cheese or hummus are classic combinations.
- Keep ready-rolled filo pastry in the freezer. As needed, add a filling and bake.
- Good quality shop-bought or home-made wholewheat or polenta cake.
- Potato salad, whole steamed baby potatoes, or pot of Russian salad (cubed potato, peas, cubed cooked carrot, a little onion, mayonnaise and vinegar). Corn fritters (small pancakes with mashed sweetcorn added to the batter before cooking) or home-made popcorn. Potato and corn are not considered vegetables but provide starches.
- Bircher Muesli: in a container put 2 tablespoons of oat flakes, chopped nuts or pine nuts, half a grated apple and some milk, soya milk or juice and seal. By lunchtime the mixture will be soft and sweet and utterly delicious.
- A good quality cereal bar (check the sugar levels). Digestives, fig rolls, a Garibaldi.
- Carrot cake, muffin, raisin loaf, chocolate brownie.
- To make bagel chips (which are a virtually salt-free substitute for crisps) slice a plain bagel into small rounds through the vertical plane. Brush the surfaces with olive oil flavoured with a little garlic paste and then grill or bake until lightly toasted. They will keep in an airtight box for two or three days.

Fruits

Fruits are rich in antioxidants and give valuable soluble fibre as well as minerals.

- Fresh fruit which is easy to handle: loose skinned satsumas, small apples, bananas, grapes off the stem, berries (blueberries, blackberries, raspberries, strawberries).
- Kiwi can be sliced in half and scooped out with a spoon, or for a fun change include physalis (Cape gooseberries or Chinese lanterns). A small pot of cubed pineapple, lychees, mango, melon, pear, plums, kiwi.
- Children will often eat fruit more enthusiastically if it is cut up into finger portions in a simple fruit salad 'lucky dip'.
- Dried fruit such as apricots, a small box of raisins, apple rings, dried figs (look out for baby figs) or dates (stoned). Trail mix (dried fruit and nuts).
- Make a fruit purée (you can use dried fruit for a stronger taste) and stir it into a yoghurt.
- Make a fruity salad more of a substantial main meal by adding cooked rice or lentils and some dried fruit to some fresh fruit salad.
- A pot of fruit purée, stewed and slightly sweetened – apple sauce is very popular and freezes in portion sizes.
- Make a milkshake in seconds (mango or other soft fruit) freeze it and let it thaw out in time for lunch.
- Fruit juice (not cordials or squashes) can be counted as one portion of fruit in a day.

Vegetables

These provide our other main sources of antioxidants as well as minerals and fibre.

- Finger food vegetables are often favoured: baby carrots or carrot sticks, cherry tomatoes, cucumber wedges, baby sweetcorn, cooked green beans, red/yellow pepper strips, steamed broccoli florets, cooked asparagus spears, raw mange tout (they taste very sweet, which is why an alternative name for them is sugar snap peas). Provide with a dip to dunk them into, such as hummus. Baby beetroot, fresh shelled peas, celery sticks stuffed with cream cheese.
- Thread alternate vegetables, fruit and cooked meat cubes on to barbecue sticks (cut off the end of the stick to make it blunt before packing) for a colourful and tasty option and provide a chutney dip.
- A small thermos of warming vegetable or tomato soup.
- If your child is 'anti-veg', find other ways to get them to eat a portion: vegetable soups for chilly winter months, vegetable juice (spicy tomato), vegetable fritters, vegetables in omelette cubes or in pasta or rice salads. Or try onion bahjis, vegetable pizzas or quiches, vegetable samosas, spring rolls and mushroom pâté.
- Small pot of coleslaw, some olives (stones removed) pickles, gherkins or a portion of sweet-tasting grilled peppers, carrot and raisin salad, cold baked beans, cold roast vegetables. Sun-dried tomato or olive purée (tapenade) spread on toast.
- Vegetable chips (parsnip, beet, carrot, sweet potatoes).

Meat or Vegetarian Alternatives

Meat provides protein, as do vegetarian alternatives, and they are rich sources of iron and zinc, both of which are needed for growing children.

- Chicken pieces in a tasty sauce, good quality sausages (85 per cent or more meat), ham or turkey strips rolled around prunes or dried apricots. Chicken or pork satay sticks (cut off sharp ends) with or without a dip, chicken tikka.
- Home-made mini chicken burgers/meatballs/fish cakes (make in advance and freeze, defrost and cook as needed).
- Eggs, hardboiled, or cubes of Spanish omelette, egg mayonnaise filling for sandwiches. Slice of quiche, devilled eggs (mash mayonnaise and mild curry flavour into the egg yolk and refill the eggs and press together again – wrap in aluminium foil to keep fresh).
- Prawn or crab salad (make sure the lunchbox will stay cool enough), tuna salad, salmon, sardines, good quality taramasalata, mackerel or salmon pâté.
- Alternatives to meat are found in the bean/nut families, and they make ideal finger foods: chickpea 'marbles', bean burgers, falafel, crackers with peanut or other nut butters (i.e. almond nut butter available from health food shops). Cold baked beans with soya sausages, hummus, a small flask of red lentil soup, tahini dip, bean salad, curried beans.

Calcium-Rich Foods

Calcium is needed for growing bones, but you can get this from a variety of sources and not just milk.

- Choose yoghurts or fromage frais. A few children's choices are free of additives and have less than 10 per cent sugar (10 g per 100 g of product). Plain 'bio' yoghurt is probably the best option as this also helps digestive health – it can be jazzed up with raisins or chopped fruit.

- Individually wrapped small cheeses are available from most supermarket pick-and-mix sections in a variety of flavours. Cream cheese or cottage cheese sandwich fillings, baby mozzarella, feta cheese.

- Other calcium-rich foods include canned sardines and salmon (mash the bones in as well), dried fruit, broccoli florets, almonds, oranges, kidney beans, blackberries, eggs, calcium-enriched flour, brown (dark) tahini. Small packets of sunflower or pumpkin seeds.

- Choose calcium-enriched alternative drinks such as soya and rice milk in small cartons. They come in all sorts of flavours which appeal to small children, such as chocolate, strawberry and banana. Calcium-enriched soya yoghurts make delicious desserts.

Drinks

It is best to limit drinks to water or milk/milk alternative drinks and to make sure that any fruit juices are drunk with meals to avoid sugars and acids in the fruit drinks damaging young teeth.

Treats

Treats are exactly what they should be, and to avoid your child guzzling sweets all day keep a sensible perspective on this whole issue. If your child is totally deprived of treats then he may want them to the exclusion of everything else. A small chocolate bar is not too bad, but if the whole box is stuffed with high sugar foods this is obviously not ideal. Aim to steer your child towards some good quality cake or oat flapjacks for dessert.

Sandwich Filling Ideas

Remember to use a variety of interesting breads to ring the changes.

- Grated cheese and grated carrot
- Tuna and sweetcorn
- Shredded chicken with redcurrant jelly
- Mashed avocado (use lemon juice to stop it browning), puréed sun-dried tomato and finely chopped spring onion
- Ham, tomato and pickle
- Egg mayonnaise and shredded lettuce
- Cheddar cheese and pesto
- Turkey and coleslaw
- Sardine and tomato
- Beans and red pepper marinated in French dressing
- Nut butter and dried apricot purée
- Hummus and chopped olives
- Cream cheese and pineapple
- Salmon and cucumber
- Cottage cheese and chopped dates
- Sausage and mango chutney
- Feta, cucumber and mint
- Vegeburger and relish in a bun

Lunchbox Planner

For inspiration, here is a three-week at-a-glance plan:

	WEEK ONE
Monday	Honey and mustard coated chicken strips (P)
	Cherry tomatoes (V)
	Oatcakes spread with raspberry jam (S)
	Satsuma (F), Yoghurt (C)
	Appletise drink – diluted (F)
Tuesday (Vegetarian)	Pot of cous cous with cooked diced vegetables (S, V)
	Hardboiled egg cut in quarters (P)
	Strawberries (F), Chocolate brownie (S)
	Water
Wednesday (Vegetarian)	Bagel with cream cheese and Marmite (S, C)
	Mini-pot baked beans (P, V)
	Kiwi chunks (F)
	Water
Thursday	Pasta twist salad with prawns, peas and diced mango (S, P, V, F)
	Grapes (F)
	Chocolate milk (C)
Friday	Sardine and tomato sandwich (P, C, V, S)
	Pear (F)
	Flapjack (S)
	Water

(S) = breads/cereals (starches/carbohydrates)

(F) = fruit

(V) = vegetables

(P) = meat or meat alternatives (proteins)

(C) = calcium-rich foods

WEEK TWO

Monday (Vegetarian)	Hummus with bagel rounds (P, C, S)
	Red pepper sticks to dip (V)
	Fromage frais (C)
	Sliced peach (F)
	Water
Tuesday	BLT sandwich (bacon, lettuce, tomato) (P, V, S)
	Pineapple cubes (F)
	Small bag of vegetable chips (carrot, beetroot, parsnip) (V)
	Banana-flavour calcium-enriched soya milk (C)
Wednesday (Vegetarian)	Salad and (dark) tahini wrap (V, C, S)
	Small packet pumpkin seeds (P, C)
	Banana (F)
	Small bar of fruit and nut chocolate
	Water
Thursday	Cream cheese dip with chopped smoked salmon (C, P)
	Pitta fingers to dip (S)
	Carrot and celery sticks to dip (V)
	Twiglets (S)
	Mango smoothie (F)
Friday	Sausage bites or ham cubes with baby sweet pickles (P, V)
	Citrus salad (orange, pink grapefruit) (F)
	Walnut muffin with extra walnuts (S, C)
	Water

WEEK THREE

Monday	Cubed turkey or chicken, sweetcorn and red pepper salad with vinaigrette (P, V)
	Berry medley (blueberries, strawberries and red grapes) (F)
	Pot of muesli and raisins soaked in milk (S, F, C)
Tuesday (Vegetarian)	Banana and raisin sandwich (F, S)
	Flask tomato soup (V)
	Small packet plain peanuts (P)
	100 per cent orange juice carton – calcium-enriched (F, C)
Wednesday	Tuna, pepper and olive pizza slices (P, V, S)
	Mini-pot of potato salad (S)
	Small packet of dried apricots (F)
	Greek yoghurt with honey (C)
	Water
Thursday	Chicken satay sticks (P)
	Mini-pot carrot and raisin salad (V, F)
	Apple crumble (F, S)
	Strawberry milk drink (C)
Friday (Vegetarian)	Bean, tomato and cheese bake (P, V, C)
	Mini-pot melon and papaya (F)
	Gingerbread man/lady (S)
	Water

Some Themes – For a Change

There are all sorts of ways in which you can make a lunchbox more interesting. You may not feel this creative on a daily basis but on occasion you can have fun with planning and make lunch more of an adventure. Also don't forget to slip something fun into the box as often as possible – a card, a picture, a photo, a message, a joke, a cartoon, a thought for the day.

Have a Shapes Day

Round Shapes Roll fillings inside a slice of bread and cut into pinwheels. Use a round cookie cutter to cut sandwiches or bits of cheese and ham. Include round crackers, cherry tomatoes, stoned olives, grapes, oranges sliced on the round, a round after-dinner chocolate mint.

Triangular Shapes Cut sandwiches into four on the diagonal. Have samosas, a triangular cheese portion, a triangular slice of cake, triangles of apple (cut into quarters and cut in half again).

Star Shapes Use a star-shaped cookie cutter to make little star-shaped biscuits and sandwiches. Have sliced starfruit, or kiwi sliced on the round (they have a starburst pattern inside). Put star stickers on a drinks cup.

Have a Colour Day

(This is not intended to include foods which rely on artificial colourings). You are unlikely to specifically plan a box like this, but if you have some leftovers in the fridge which suggest a theme then it can be fun to put together.

Pink/Red Box Prawn pizza slices, cherry tomatoes, red pepper rings, strawberry yoghurt, red grapes, cooled fruit tea.

Green and Blue Box Green beans, cucumber and baby potato salad in vinaigrette, green omelette (made with peas and chopped parsley), cup of watercress soup, mini blue cheese cubes, water.

Yellow Box Egg mayonnaise sandwich, little box of saffron rice and sweetcorn salad, yellow pepper, satsuma, banana milk.

Have a National Theme Day

Indian Chickpea curry, meat paratha (meat stuffed flatbread), onion bhaji, fresh fruit cubes (orange, mango, pineapple), carton of orange juice.

Italian Italian flag salad (baby mozzarella, halved cherry tomatoes, green beans), ciabatta bread, little pot of tiramisu, grapes, cooled red fruit tea (pretend it's red wine).

French Brie, baguette, salad petit pois (peas and tomato), walnuts (very French), gâteau au fraise (strawberry cake), bottle of French mineral water.

Celebration Box

Make up special boxes for birthdays, Easter, Jewish New Year, Diwali, Chinese New Year or other celebrations.

Lunchbox Questions

Is mayonnaise safe in sandwiches on a hot summer's day or might it go off?

Commercial mayonnaise should last through until lunchtime as long as it is kept at a reasonably cool temperature, though home-made mayonnaise, using raw eggs, is more likely to go off. Check lunch-boxes are not being stored on a shelf in direct sunlight, or over a radiator in winter (not unheard of!). You can freeze the drink you put in your child's box – by lunchtime it will have defrosted and will have kept the contents of the box cool all morning (wrap the drink container in a plastic bag to stop condensation making other food soggy).

How do I get round the fact that fruit or cut up veg just come back uneaten?

Fruit and veg can be disguised, for example offering thick Spanish omelette cubes or a delicious soup in a small flask. Remember that fun food need not be junk food: there are healthier fruit and veg snack options which children love, such as banana chips (fibre and potassium) and 'moist' dried apricots (antioxidants and fibre).

Is it OK to have the same old ham sandwiches day after day?

Ham is ideal for protein and is rich in iron and zinc for growing bodies. If you ensure the bread is wholemeal you will also provide fibre, calcium, magnesium and B-vitamins. Children get by amazingly well eating the same food day in, day out, so don't worry – their taste fads will change a few months from now anyway. Make sure that you vary the diet as much as possible at home.

My child has turned vegetarian, do you have any lunchbox ideas?

Vegetarian children grow up just as healthy, as long as they have a well-balanced diet. Meat is rich in iron and zinc, which growing bodies need, and the main vegetarian choices which provide these are beans, pulses, nuts and seeds. Eggs and soya products have an excellent balance of most nutrients and dairy products are rich in calcium – so a child can be well nourished without eating meat. Hummus is a delicious dip, while falafel, pizza slices (wholemeal is best), vegeburgers and soya sausages, cut into bite-sized chunks, are all good choices. In a rush, a tub of cottage cheese with pineapple or chives and crackers to scoop it up is a good standby, but if you have more time make up a stuffed taco or savoury rice with leftover chopped vegetables and beans, adding some salsa for moistness.

I'm on a tight budget – do you have any economical lunchbox ideas?

The most expensive choices are actually the 'convenience' options. Having said that, it is true that a piece of fruit is often more expensive than a few economy-pack biscuits, so it can be a challenge to work out how to provide a healthy box. In reality, inexpensive 'healthy' eating often needs more preparation time, which is why it is a good idea to make full use of your freezer. Rice, lentils (which make delicious soups), beans (make into dips or add to vegetables such as chopped tomatoes and French dressing to make yummy salads), wholegrain flour for baking, fruit in season (make fruit cobblers and freeze) are all really cheap and can be made into many delicious dishes.

Milk and Dairy

Standard advice is that children need to drink milk. But that is not strictly true. What is desirable is that children achieve a certain intake of calcium daily. Obviously one of the easiest ways to do this is to drink a pint-a-milk-a-day. Whichever type of milk is drunk, 100 g provides around 115 mg of calcium daily. The guidelines say:

- Under 1 year old babies need breast or formula milk, around 1 pint/0.5 litre daily (under one year of age a child must not be given ordinary milk).
- At 1–2 years they need full-fat cow's milk, around ⅔ pint/0.35 litre daily.
- Between 2–5 years they can have semi-skimmed milk if desired, ½ pint/0.25 litre daily is recommended.
- Children of 5 years and older can move on to skimmed milk, if desired.

Suggested Figures for Calcium

	EARs (Estimated Average Requirements)	RNIs (Reference Nutrient Intakes)[*]
1–3 years	275 mg	350 mg
4–6 years	350 mg	450 mg
7–10 years	425 mg	550 mg
11–18 years, male	750 mg	1000 mg
11–18 years, female	625 mg	800 mg

[*]The RNIs provide for a margin of error over the EARs

But for children with a dairy allergy or intolerance (more about the difference in a moment) drinking milk can lead to health problems. Only about 2 per cent of children are believed to have a true food allergy, however many more have intolerances.

A great worry for parents is that their child will suffer dietary deficiencies by avoiding milk, cheese and yoghurt. But not all of these products need to be avoided all the time – it is a question of knowing what is likely to be the problem and how best to address it.

There has been a steep increase in conditions such as asthma, glue ear and eczema in childhood. These ailments can all be due, in part, to a high quantity and frequency of dairy intake. In a small number of children problems can start early on when a child is sensitised to milk protein when breastfed as the mother is including milk and cheese in her diet. Most often symptoms of allergy start when children are given formula milk or are introduced to milk or cheese in their own diet. A major contributor to this might be the timing of introducing formula. While 70 per cent of mothers breast feed (an improvement from 50 per cent 50 years ago) the majority only do so for six weeks, instead of the recommended six months minimum. The gut of a six-week-old baby is more prone to being sensitive to cow's milk proteins than is a six-month-old baby. It is also possible for an allergy or intolerance to develop at a much later stage, which is confusing for parents when a staple food, which was fine, suddenly causes problems

Dairy products were only introduced into the human diet around 10,000 years ago, which is the blink of an eye in evolutionary terms. Around 70 per cent of the world's adult population lacks the milk-digesting enzyme lactase making it difficult for them to consume dairy products. This deficiency is particularly prevalent amongst those of African, Asian, Southern American, Jewish and Mediterranean descent. In many people, their levels of lactase decline from around the age of two or three – which presumably is around the time that Mother Nature decides we should be fully weaned and on a mixed diet providing sufficient calcium. Yet we remain the only animals on earth who continue to drink milk after that age by drinking the milk of other species.

Calcium Concerns

If your child has to cut back on dairy products, calcium is available from a wide variety of foods. In fact, drinking milk often curbs appetite (see Appetite Squashers, page 10) which in turn means that a child does not have any interest in eating from a wide variety of foods. This means that a vicious cycle develops of falling back more heavily on milk for sustenance. Heavy milk intake has also been partly blamed for the epidemic of iron-deficiency anaemia we are now seeing in children, because milk is a poor source of iron and drinking milk reduces intake of other foods which are rich in iron. Peak bone mass is achieved in the first 30 years of life and calcium intake in childhood is an important contributor to this, but it is not the only one. Calcium loss from the body is also important (it is leached out of the bones and is excreted in urine) and affects overall calcium balance. Many dietary habits that children have, including drinking colas and other sodas and high salt intake, encourages calcium loss. It is also evident that having a good fruit and vegetable intake is much more important for bone health than was previously believed. Children absorb calcium from foods much more efficiently than adults – the hormone regulation of their guts ensures this – and slightly lower intakes of calcium in the diet actually promote increased absorption of calcium. Therefore it may not be calcium intake that is the only important thing, but that limiting calcium loss is just as important. To quote the Department of Health book on *Dietary Reference Values in the UK*, 'several populations of the world consume calcium levels lower than the current RDA [Recommended Daily Allowance] for the UK yet show no evidence of adverse effects'. For calcium intake recommendations for different age groups *see* page 163.

This one day menu will provide around 600 mg of calcium, suitable for ten years or under. For older children, increase portion sizes or add calcium-enriched dairy alternatives or a little cheese or yoghurt or milk in puddings.

2 eggs
handful of dates
1 orange
1 carrot
$\frac{1}{2}$ portion broccoli spears
sunflower seeds
$\frac{1}{2}$ small tin pink salmon
1 calcium-enriched soya yoghurt
2 slices wholemeal bread, spread with dark tahini
1 portion baked beans
fruit salad (for example, kiwi and melon)

- Calcium is best transported into bones with vitamin D. The best source of this in the summertime is half an hour to one hour of exposure to sunlight, which causes the skin to make vitamin D – another good reason to run around out of doors. In the winter, the best sources are dietary, from oily fish, fish oils, margarines (which must be fortified by law), fortified cereals and fortified milks.

Children up to the age of three are advised to supplement 7 mcg daily. If a child is confined indoors and not exposed to sunlight, then 7–10 mcg supplementation daily may be necessary. Children with dark skins who are less efficient at making vitamin D, are particularly at risk, especially if they cover up when out of doors.

- Calcium is also best consumed with magnesium. While dairy products are rich sources of calcium they only offer tiny amounts of magnesium. Foods rich in both calcium and magnesium are all green leafy vegetables (the green compound chlorophyll contains magnesium), nuts and seeds. (Cows and goats do not grow healthy bones by just drinking milk – they eat grass, a rich source of calcium and magnesium packed chlorophyll.)

- Some mineral waters (choose a low-sodium brand), and even tap water from hard water areas, contribute significant amounts of calcium – up to 10 per cent of intake.

- The most sensible approach is to make sure your child eats a variety of foods and doesn't depend on any one food group. If you are cutting out one type of food, such as dairy products, make sure that calcium-rich substitutes are included in the diet.

Symptoms Linked to Dairy Sensitivity

- Asthma
- Catarrh
- Constipation
- Dark circles beneath eyes
- Diabetes
- Diarrhoea
- Eczema
- Bloating
- Flatulence
- Glue ear
- Hay fever
- Headaches
- Upper respiratory tract infections

There are two main causes of dairy sensitivity: lactose and proteins. Lactose intolerance, as a result of a lack of or insufficient lactase, is the simplest to recognise. The lactose, which is milk sugar, is not digested and is left in the gut to ferment. This leads to side effects such as uncomfortable wind and bloating – the milk sugar is literally brewing up a storm. Some lactose intolerant people can drink some milk and be OK but have a threshold of intake beyond which it becomes troublesome.

There are more than 30 proteins in cow's milk. Casein is the protein most significantly linked to allergy. It is a large molecule which is so dense that the amount is reduced in formula milk to more closely mimic breast milk. It is really designed for a calf's digestive system rather than a human child's and it takes quite a lot of work to break them down. Goat's milk contains a different type of casein which is less linked to allergy and is easier to digest and so better tolerated.

Many children will grow out of a dairy intolerance over time – their bodies seem to adapt. This, at least, is the conventional viewpoint. Another viewpoint is that one lot of symptoms, such as eczema or asthma, abate or resolve – usually when approaching teen years – only to reappear in a different form later on. It is common to see 30–40 year olds who are stressed and tired and who are reporting other allergy/sensitivity problems such as migraines or irritable bowel syndrome. On questioning they commonly have had dairy allergy or intolerance problems in childhood which eventually cleared up.

What You Can Do About It

- Usually it is sufficient to just cut back on dairy products – to limit your child, say, to cheese once a week, to yoghurts twice a week and a drop of milk in tea or the occasional dessert.
- If your child is lactose intolerant, skimmed milk or semi-skimmed is worse than whole milk as there is proportionately more milk sugar.
- Lactose-free milk is available in large supermarkets.
- Lactase enzymes can easily be found in pharmacies or health food shops. One brand is Colief Infant Drops (0800 522 8243

www.colief.com). Adding a few drops to milk a hour or so before consumption will give them enough time to act and break down the lactose (the milk is noticeably much sweeter as a result).

- Hard cheese usually does not cause problems for lactose intolerance as there is little lactose left in it.

- Good quality yoghurts which have been fermented for long enough (the plain bio-yoghurts should be fine) will have little lactose as the bacteria used in their preparation have pre-digested the milk sugar.

- Butter is usually well tolerated as it is just fat (with a few stray protein and lactose molecules in it – your child has to be very sensitive to react). However, as it is just fat it does not count as a dairy portion and it has no calcium in it.

- Goat's milk is often much better tolerated if sensitive to cow's milk proteins. It is available from good supermarkets and health food shops and it does not taste 'funny'. St Hellens Farm produce milk, yoghurts and cheeses (01430 861 715 www.sthelens-farm.co.uk). However, goat's milk has just as much lactose in it as does cow's milk.

- Calcium-enriched soya milk, rice milk and oat milk are all widely available. Many children with cow's milk allergy or sensitivity are brought up quite happily on these products (including my son who drank rice milk). They are not suitable before one year of age and should be a part of a balanced, mixed diet.

- With the advent of 'functional foods' – everyday foods which have some added nutritional content (and are often therefore a bit more expensive) – you can buy calcium-enriched fruit juices. A 250 ml glass will give a child half of their daily calcium requirement.

- If your child has a serious cow's milk protein allergy, you will need to avoid foods which, in addition to milk, cream, cheese, butter and yoghurt, contain the following:

– buttermilk	– ghee
– casein/caseinate	– lactalbumin

- crème fra^che   - lactic acid
- curds   - lactobacillus
- kefir   - lactoglobulin
- lactose   - quark
- protein-enriched foods (this could mean milk protein)
- rennet   - whey

Munchies

Snack times can be challenging. On the one hand you have a child who obviously needs a top-up, and on the other, you might feel that you would rather your child does not eat something that will interfere with appetite at the next meal. Faced with a full-on nag it is also easy to give in to pleas for crisps and sweets. But if you always keep healthy snacks to hand then it really doesn't matter if appetite is a little blunted at meal times because the snack has been nutritious. It is only if the snack is a nutritional disaster area and appetite at meal times is also affected that the whole thing becomes counter-productive. It's also an idea to be prepared in the car when going on a longish journey so you are not waylaid by the junk in petrol station shops. Children are usually starving when they get out of school so having a snack to hand is ideal, and helps reduce the average £6 per child per week spent on the way home from school – that's £365m per year – mainly on crisps, sweets and fizzy drinks. And just to prove they don't need these foods, in recent years the figures have changed as kids spend more of their money on trading cards and mobile phone top-ups.

Healthy Snack Ideas

- An oatcake on its own or with nut butter.
- Half an avocado with a few prawns.

- Dried apple rings or raisins with a few nuts.
- Rye cracker with cottage cheese or hummus.
- Cheese cubes with grapes.
- A small packet of corn chips with salsa dip.
- A chunk of banana or orange frozen on a stick is refreshing and fun.
- A fruit scone or banana muffin.
- Vegetable sticks or breadsticks with dips such as hummus, guacamole, mushroom pâté, tzatziki or mackerel pâté.
- Dried or fresh fruit with cottage cheese.
- A yoghurt lolly.
- A mashed banana piled on some rye toast and sprinkled with cinnamon.
- A yoghurt topped with flaked coconut and chopped dried apricots.
- Strips of ham wrapped around prunes.
- A cup of warming soup (fresh soups are available in cartons).
- Wholemeal toast fingers with cream cheese and pineapple.
- A slice of fruit loaf.
- Mini rice cakes and a cheese stick.
- Bruchetta – toasted bread (ciabatta is best) brushed with olive oil and garlic and topped with chopped fresh tomato and shredded basil leaf or spread with tapenade (olive or sun-dried tomato paste available from supermarkets).

Substitutions

One way to improve the picture is to make easy substitutions of one snack for another. These are some healthier options that your child probably won't even notice:

Crisps

- Breadsticks (even better with a dip such as avocado, salsa or hummus).
- Twiglets, although fairly high in salt, but no more so than crisps, are lower in fat, plus they are wholemeal and a good source of B-vitamins.
- Nuts of all sorts are good sources of polyunsaturated fats, fibre and minerals. Unsalted is best.
- Oatcakes are moreish and have good fibre levels which regulate blood sugar.
- Japanese rice crackers.
- Blue corn chips, available from health food shops and large supermarkets, are better than the average crisp.
- Flavoured rice cakes are now widely available and are not as high in fat.

Biscuits

- Wholemeal digestive biscuits (delicious with a sliver of cheese).
- Garibaldi biscuits and fig rolls have useful amounts of dried fruit in them.

Chocolate

- Offer a higher cocoa content chocolate than the types typically available. Green & Black do the best ones in my view, but there are others.

Cake

- Fruit muffins.
- Carrot cake.
- Oat and raisin flapjacks.

Nutrition Needs

Children's nutritional needs are important to recognise. There are several essential things to remember. Children need sufficient calories to grow and thrive and low-fat, adult diets do not achieve this. Low-fat diets are also often deficient in the vitamins and minerals children need for optimal development. For this reason, restricted calorie intake is rarely appropriate.

But just any old fats won't do – what children need are healthy sources of fats. These seem to be particularly vital for children and a shortage can lead to problems with mental function, eye and skin health, and asthma.

Children's growth means that they need a concentrated source of particular nutrients. Those necessary for bone health and mental development are of particular importance. For more information on this, *see* Vitamins and Minerals, page 251. The best way to achieve a plentiful source is to ensure a varied and interesting diet, but, of course, this is the one thing that children tend not to be getting these days.

If you are educating your child about food, understanding some of the basic terms can help. The basic components of food are as follows:

Proteins

These are needed for growth and repair of body tissues. They are found in meat, fish, eggs, cheese, pulses (beans, lentils and other legumes), nuts and seeds. While animal sources of protein are considered 'first class', because they provide a balance of amino acids (the building blocks that make up proteins), plant sources are just as good, as long as your child gets a variety of different types (and plant sources also has the added advantage of providing fibre in the diet). Children need at least one portion of protein daily from animal sources (meat, fish, eggs) or if vegetarian or vegan, two portions daily from meat alternatives such as beans, other pulses, nuts and seeds. Even if your family is not vegetarian, aiming to have two or three plant protein-based meals a week is a good thing as they are high in fibre and low in saturated fats.

Carbohydrates

These are used for energy of all sorts – to work and play, to build body tissues, to grow, and to think (the brain uses a third of energy). There are two main types of carbohydrates – starches and sugars. Starches are simply made up from long lines of sugars linked together. After digestion, all useable carbohydrates from starches are turned into blood sugar. The main difference between the carbohydrates is how easily they are converted into blood sugar and the length of time this takes. Generally speaking, slow is better than fast, as it gives more sustained energy over time. Slow-releasing carbohydrates are found in wholegrains (brown rice, rye), porridge oats, barley, pulses and beans, and vegetables. Potatoes, sweet potatoes, parsnips and fruit are other good sources of carbohydrates because they are all rich in various vitamins and minerals needed for optimum health. Fast-releasing carbohydrates are found in refined grains (white bread, white rice), corn, sugar and sugary foods and drinks. Carbohydrate starches (but not sugars) also provide fibre, which is needed for healthy bowels and to regulate blood sugar levels.

Fats

These are used for energy. Special types of fats – polyunsaturated fats – are also used for growth and development, for nervous tissue, hormone production and building cell membranes. Fats in general are needed for fuel, to aid the absorption of fat soluble vitamins, and to contribute taste and texture to food. So they do have important functions, but a balance is needed to make sure we get the right sort, and don't overdo the non-beneficial fats.

- Saturated fats are solid at room temperature (such as fat found around meat, butter and lard, the fat suspended in full-fat milk and cream). Too much saturated fat in the diet is linked to health problems, such as heart disease.
- Hydrogenated trans-fats are artificially manufactured fats that resemble saturated fats, and they have been linked to cancer and heart disease. Because of their plastic-like qualities, they allow for 'crispiness' of baked goods and are thus found in cakes, biscuits and pastry, as well as cheaper margarines. They are potentially the cause of problems because they have no biological activity and are high in trans-fats, which are also unhealthy, and so it is best if their intake is limited. New regulations are now being set in some countries about maximum amounts in foods.

Positive health benefits are associated with monounsaturated fats and polyunsaturated fats.

Monounsaturates are mainly found in olive oil and it is probably their role in displacing saturated fats, when used, for example, in cooking, that means they are a healthier option.

Polyunsaturated fats are found in vegetable, seed and nut oils, as well as seeds, nuts and oily fish. They are often referred to as omega-6s and omega-3s and are essential for good health. However, because they do not have a long shelf-life they are not used as much as saturates and hydrogenates in processed and packaged foods. This is one of the reasons why cooking from fresh ingredients is a healthier option (the other reasons being that overall fat intake, salt and sugar levels can be kept in balance). Particularly important polyunsaturates for human health are those found in oily fish, from the omega-3 family of fatty acids.

Omega-6 are found in most nuts, for example walnuts, pecans, brazils, pine nuts, peanuts, cashews; seeds, for example sesame, sunflower, pumpkin; and the oils of these nuts and seeds and also grains, including the margarines made from these oils (though beware of those also made with hydrogenated fats).

Omega-3 are found in fewer common dietary sources: flax oil, linseeds, canola (rape) oil, walnuts and its oil, soya, (soya oil is best avoided as extraction uses high heat and chemicals), hemp seeds and oil; as well as oily fish, for example mackerel, tuna (not canned), sardines, salmon, sprats, whitebait, pink trout and oysters. Ideally, children need to eat two portions of fish a week, of which one needs to be oily fish. Any oils should be virgin pressed, purchased in dark bottles and stored in a cool cupboard or the fridge. Nuts and seeds should be unsalted, and either ground or in butter form for young children (assuming, of course, they don't suffer from allergies).

Vitamin and Minerals These are found in small quantities in the food we eat and are essential for health. Deficiencies can lead to serious health problems. All foods (apart from sugar) provide vitamins and minerals, however some foods are better sources than others. For more detailed information, *see* Vitamins and Minerals, page 251.

Water Much of our water comes from food and not from the tap. High water content foods, such as fruits and vegetables, are associated with good health. For more information, *see* Water, page 270.

Obesity

The idealised childhood, now found only in nostalgic novels, involves scraped knees from shinning up trees, fishing down at the creek and full bellies from scrumping apples. A more typical modern childhood centres on eating takeaway burger and chips while slumped in front of the telly watching improbably skinny pop stars doing their thing, followed by an hour or so shooting down space monsters on a computer game.

This change in habits has, inevitably, lead to changes in childhood health. Over the last 10 to 20 years it has become apparent that sedentary lifestyles, poor food choices and eating disorders are contributing to soaring obesity and anorexia statistics in children. Children naturally come in all shapes and sizes. If you are concerned about your child, however, you need to inform yourself. Obesity in childhood has been linked to increased risk of heart disease and diabetes in adult years. The fatty deposits that are implicated in heart disease are often found in the arteries of pre-school children.

Children have increasingly become prisoners in their own homes as parents are worried about letting them outside to play unsupervised and, of course, they generally no longer walk or cycle to school. Between 1985 and 1992 the average distance children walked each year fell by one-fifth (50 miles) and children were cycling 10 miles a year less than previously. In the meantime, car miles travelled by children have shot up by 40 per cent. The explosion in the sale of children's videos and computer games is evidence that their lifestyles are changing.

The number of British toddlers who are becoming tubbier is also escalating. In the last ten years, the number of overweight children under the age of four increased from one-sixth to one-quarter, while obesity doubled to nearly one in ten. One in five ten-year-old girls, and one in eight boys in Britain is overweight. Yet during this same period the number of calories that the typical child consumes seems to have gone down by a couple of hundred calories a day (although this is debated). This is not just a UK problem, but a Western problem, with similar findings in France, Sweden and Finland. The inevitable conclusion is that it is reduced physical activity that is a major factor in obesity.

So if calorie intake has been dropping how might diet affect obesity? Well the sources of calories eaten could be making an impact. Eating foods which are poor providers of necessary nutrients, i.e. vitamins and minerals, is going to affect overall health and energy levels. If a child is energy depleted – the most obvious example would be if they were a little bit anaemic (iron deficient), though this could relate to other nutrients, such as vitamin C and B-vitamins – it is not going to be easy for them to summon up the energy and interest to be active. This has not been studied yet, but to my mind makes a lot of sense.

How to Work Out if Your Child Has a Genuine Weight Problem

For children, the calculations are age-plotted on a centile chart. For these, check out www.keepkidshealthy.com for a paediatric's guide to children's health with a BMI (body mass index) calculator or www.paediatrics.about.com/-cs/growthcharts2/ for growth charts for babies and children. If you are not on the internet, your doctor's surgery should be able to provide charts. Adult BMI charts are not appropriate for children.

What to Do to Help Your Child

- Indulge in weekend sports as a family. Join clubs for martial arts, football, tennis and swimming. Children need at least one hour of physical activity each day. If they are not getting this at school, concentrate on active after school pursuits or get involved in running a sports club at the school. Do these on a rota basis with other parents to make it manageable.
- Cut back on sedentary activities – limit TV and computer games to 30–60 minutes on school days and 60–90 minutes daily during weekends and holidays.
- Weight problems in parents are a risk factor for obesity and so you may need to look at your own exercise and eating habits.
- It is important to maintain self-esteem so that a child does not develop a complex about food. Rather than putting a child on an adult-tailored slimming diet, which is usually inappropriate as it can lack essential nutrients, it is more helpful to encourage him to focus on healthy eating.

- Some substitutions can improve the picture. Breakfasts are often sugary, so try offering some toast, home-made pancakes, porridge or a boiled egg on occasion to break the habit. At age two, you can switch to semi-skimmed milk. Snacks for the school playground could include Twiglets, raisins or a mini-sandwich. Don't stop them having chips at school (this is, anyway, impractical), instead encourage them to have a smaller helping while increasing the serving of healthier foods.

- Vegetables you can easily prepare individually include green beans, broccoli or cauliflower florets, raw carrot sticks or baby tomatoes.

- Leaner take-away options could include a grilled chicken kebab or a child's pizza with half the cheese.

- Baked desserts that feature fruit, such as crumbles, pies and cobblers, may be a painless way of getting them to eat fruit, especially if they have a sweet tooth.

- Concentrate on healthy eating at home and remember that if you keep lots of crisps, sweets and cordials in the cupboard those are what will be eaten. The Rainbow Food Chart (available from 01273 703 461) is an excellent way to make a child-friendly game out of eating the advised five portions of fruit and vegetables daily, or make your own chart (see Projects and Activities, page 207).

- Educate your child to make healthier choices in the school canteen – look at the menus together and discuss the choices or work out healthy packed lunches.

- Having no structure for family meals can lead to disordered eating habits so make it a priority to eat regularly with your children.

- Snacking on low-nutrient foods that displace healthier foods is a frequent problem. Sugary cordials, squashes, colas and juice drinks are the worst offenders. Offer water instead.

See also Disordered Eating, page 49 and Exercise and Sport, page 61.

Organic Eating

We currently spend £400m a year in the UK on organic food, and a tenfold rise is predicted in the next five to ten years. There are many different reasons why we are increasingly embracing this method of food production. Food scares such as salmonella and E.coli contamination, BSE and GM foods have created a highly suspicious food customer. Parents, in particular, are often concerned about the levels of pesticides used on crops which may have adverse health consequences for their children. Many buyers are committed to buying organic foods as a means of protecting the environment or improving conditions for farm animals. Other buyers believe that organic produce has the edge because, to them, it tastes better.

Whatever the reasons, this now translates into a huge market. The demand has grown so much that we are currently in the situation where 70 per cent of the UK's organic food is imported. This high level of imports begs questions about whether we are likely to see a dilution of standards. Organic food in supermarkets is sold pre-packaged so that it can't be confused with non-organic. The Soil Association (UK5) licences 70 per cent of UK grown organic food and you can look out for their logo. Other certification includes UKROFS – UK Register of Organic Food Standards – (UK1). Other codes are UK2–UK8, which encompass bodies such as the Scottish Organic Producers and the Irish Organic Farmers. Imported foods from outside the EU have to apply for certification from a European organic body, who do an Equivalence Check to make sure that foods are grown in accordance with EU standards.

The rules governing what constitutes organic food are specific. Some of these rules are:

- No use of artificial fertilisers.
- No use of artificial food colouring to the final product.

- No use of preservatives in the final product – other than sodium nitrates and nitrites approved for use in cured bacon and ham.
- No growth promoters in the rearing of animals.
- Antibiotics used only for treatment and not as a prophylactic or as a growth enhancer.
- Tight animal welfare guidelines.
- No genetically modified ingredients.

Health Benefits

The latest government study of non-organic produced foods found pesticide residues in nearly a 27 per cent of foods overall and in fruits and vegetables the number of contaminated samples had gone up to from 33 per cent to 43 per cent. Even 11 per cent of baby foods have pesticide residues in them. Government spokespeople will always mention that the majority of these residues are well within the safe limits which have been set. The main criticism of this stance, by people such as Professor John Wargo, author of *Our Children's Toxic Legacy*, is that little is known of the cumulative effects of eating a cocktail of different residues, particularly on the bodies of small children. Organic food has proved itself in the eyes of many purchasers by not being subject to many of the food scares that have come to a head in the last three decades. To date, there have been no cases of BSE in totally organic beef herds. Chemicals now banned generally, such as the organochlorines DDT and Lindane, have *never* been used in organic food production at all. Likewise, antibiotics, the over use of which is likely to be contributing significantly to the birth of the 'superbug', are only used (as they should be) for medicinal purposes, and not as growth promoters.

Safety Scares

We have, of course, seen recent newspaper headlines about the danger of contamination of organic food by E.coli 0157, the strain responsible for many poisoning cases. This was supposed to be because manure is used in organic farming. The statistics, which sparked off this alarm, came from the only year, 1996, when organic foods were implicated in an E.coli outbreak and they were lumped together with 'natural' foods. Seventy-one people became sick after drinking unpasteurised 'natural' apple juice (not organic), and 61 people from eating organic lettuce. On investigation, the lettuce preparation area had become contaminated by the run-off from a neighbouring, conventional dairy farm. Animal manure is actually in use in both organic and conventional farming, but only organic standards specify composting procedures and that manure must be kept away from fruit and vegetables.

Organic Junk Food?

Your child can eat an organic junk food diet just as easily as a non-organic junk food diet, and fresh foods need never pass your child's lips. Packaged foods provide high profit margins, which means that manufacturers are keen to jump on the bandwagon. They can also be very seductive to the buyer for many reasons, not least of all convenience, but it may be best to reserve your organic purchasing power for fresh foods. Organic sugar and white flour products are really not worth buying from a health perspective (there are environmental arguments), and it is pretty safe to say that ignoring some products such as organic sweets and organic doughnuts, is the best policy.

It is well worth reading the labels – don't assume that because it says organic that it is healthier. For instance, some organic cereals have more sugar or salt than the non-organic versions, and this is true of other products. There are, however, some good quality convenience-food producers who aim their products at the children's market and who are interested in the ethical issues surrounding our children's food (such as giving them good quality ingredients). They make familiar convenience, but organic and additive-free, foods such as burgers, sausages, pizzas, cornflakes and other foods. These include Organix Foods, who make frozen convenience foods, Pure Organics with their 'For Georgia's sake' range of frozen foods (designed to help the owners' autistic child's need for an additive-free diet), and Whole Earth Foods, who make a wide range of familiar packet, bottled and canned organic foods.

Nutrition and Taste Benefits

Recently, newspapers have jumped on the widely held belief that organic foods are supposed to taste better, and indeed taste tests have shown mixed results. Some individual studies show that organic foods taste better, but plenty don't. Because of their lower water content, organic vegetables tend to hold their shape better, and so taste better, when cooked, than conventional vegetables, which can often turn mushy. Other food groups, however, and particularly processed foods, may not necessarily taste better. Organic chickens perform well on the taste test because their better living conditions and greater amount of exercise means their meat is less fatty and stronger tasting.

You can get tasteless organic foods as well as tasteless non-organic produce, and you may need to persevere to find suppliers, shops or brands that you like. I have made a number of converts to eating organic vegetables and meat in my area when I have served them to friends who subsequently signed up to the local box scheme (and this includes a few spouses of farmers who farm conventionally!). Box scheme information is available from The Soil Association. By signing up to the scheme, you can do your bit to support local UK farmers who have made the investment to convert to organic production.

There have also been questions raised about whether organic food is nutritionally more beneficial than non-organic produce. There is no definitive answer to this – some tests have shown for and some against. We have, however, seen a drop in the nutritional content of conventionally produced foods since the Second World War (before which organic-type production was the norm and not the exception) and there really needs to be better and more comprehensive testing than has been done to date.

Cost

Another issue for many families is the question of cost. There is no doubt that, on average, organic foods cost more than non-organic. As the yields on organic farms are less than on non-organic, precisely because they don't use intensive rearing and try to squeeze every last gasp out of the land, this is likely to remain the case for the foreseeable future. However, the margins in supermarkets do sometimes seem to be disproportionately high, and, again, a less expensive basket can usually be obtained by shopping around and using local suppliers. Another way to cut back on cost is to avoid stocking up with convenience foods and to cook more from scratch, using cheaper, in season, produce and focussing more on inexpensive beans, pulses and grains. For more information, and advice, contact:

- The Soil Association (0117 929 0661 or www.soilassociation.org), who are the main licensing body for organic produce in the UK. They can supply details of your nearest organic farms and of local box delivery schemes. Supporting local growers reduces the dependence on imported organic produce.

- Organic Consumers Association (www.purefood.com) and Organic Europe (www.organic-europe.net).
- Read *The Little Food Book* by Craig Sams, a must-read, common sense book which explores important food issues.

Get Chemicals Out of Your Child's Life

- Buy organic food wherever possible. Organic meat, milk, chocolate and other fatty foods are particularly important.
- Choose chemical-free shampoos and toothpastes from suppliers such as Green People (01444 401 444 or www.greenpeople.co.uk).
- Avoid organophosphate laced head-lice lotions. (A study by the Health and Safety Executive established that they can put children five times over the safety limits and repeated use can damage the nervous system). Use lice combs with conditioner and see Home Remedy Kit, page 102, for suggestions on treatment.
- Avoid plastic wrapping and packaging on fatty foods such as bacon, cheese and prepared dishes. They leach phenolic compounds. Buy sliced bacon, for example, and have it wrapped in waxed paper.
- Avoid chemical treatments around the house and garden: flea treatments for pets, wood treatments, garden pesticides.
- Parks and playing fields are regularly sprayed. If you use one frequently, find out what your local council's spraying schedule is.

Outdoor Eating

Children love to eat out of doors, so much so that even ordinary teatime fare, spread out on a blanket in the garden, or even better in a tent or tepee, can transform the meal into an adventure and encourage them not only to eat all their food up but to try new things as well. Picnics needn't just mean soggy sandwiches, and barbecues don't have to mean burnt sausages and undercooked drumsticks. Outdoor eating can be viewed as an opportunity to get creative.

Involving your children in the planning of your excursions or barbecues can also be great fun. Children can be involved in packing the picnic basket or in preparing some of the food, threading vegetables and meat on skewers for the barbecue (warn them about the sharp ends) or helping to make up a delicious fruit salad.

Summertime Picnic Food

- Instead of the usual sandwiches choose from the range of interesting breads, such as sun-dried tomato ciabatta, rosemary foccacia, naan, chapattis, onion bagels or tortilla wraps.
- A great way to use up leftovers, such as roasted vegetables, is to combine them with couscous, which takes 5 minutes to make, and toss with a vinaigrette. Or mix chopped tomato, cucumber, spring onions, fresh mint and feta cheese with couscous and add dressing.
- Instead of dealing with fiddly cutlery you could plan menus of finger-food only. For example: mini-quiches, chunks of cheese and ripe tomatoes with French bread, sliced vegetables, bunches of grapes, or just take a (thoroughly) cooked chicken, pull off sections and eat with luscious tomatoes or mild radishes.

- Sweet treats can still be healthy. Sliced banana bread, malt bread or muffins, banana chips, boxed raisins, a large bowl of mixed berries, a small watermelon to slice, or a refreshing citrus fruit salad are all great choices.

Barbecue Ideas

- Lamb and mint patties or pork and apple burgers (*see* page 40 for how to make these). Or make these into sausage shapes and thread on to skewers.
- Kebabs can be made from a variety of ingredients (brush with oil before cooking), including chicken or lamb chunks interspersed with firm fruit chunks such as apple, pear or pineapple, or bacon rolls, mushrooms and dried apricots. If using fish, make sure it is a firm textured fish such as monkfish, salmon, or tuna. Or make vegetable kebabs, – alternating the colours using red, green and yellow peppers, mushrooms, baby sweetcorn, quartered onions, and firm textured tofu (best if marinaded, *see* below).
- Make your own delicious barbecue marinades. These can be made in minutes and turn chicken, meat or fish into a princely feast. Marinate in the fridge for at least 30 minutes but ideally for 2 hours. The following are just a few ideas:

  - Honey, mustard (Dijon grain is best), and olive oil (great with sausages or lamb chops)
  - Balsamic vinegar, olive oil, garlic
  - Puréed tomato, onion, red pepper, paprika and olive oil
  - Bio-yoghurt, lemon, garlic, mint and olive oil (yoghurt also tenderises meat marinaded in it)
  - Herby olive oil with garlic, rosemary and sage
- Other fun foods to cook on the barbecue are corn on the cob (keep the husks on until they are cooked and serve with melted

butter), bananas (bake in their skin until black, let them cool for a bit before peeling and serve with Greek yoghurt), and jacket potatoes (pre-bake these for a while then put on the barbecue to crisp up).

Summer Eating Safety Tips

Warm months mean that extra attention needs to be paid to food safety and outdoor health hazards.

- When buying food remember that the temperature in the boot of your car can get warm enough to multiply bacteria which, if the food is not then cooked properly, can lead to food poisoning. Keep a coolbag in the back of the car for items such as meat, fish, cheese, milk, pâtés, fresh dips and sauces. Thoroughly cook any dishes you are packing for your picnic.
- Keep food cool. Ideally, chill it in your fridge first and pack in cool boxes with ice packs. Carton drinks can also be chilled to keep the temperature down.
- Some foods, such as shellfish, fresh fish, unpasteurised cheeses and mayonnaise are particularly prone to going off, so it may be best to avoid taking them for picnics unless you are sure you can keep them cool.
- Not only is it unappealing to have barbecue food which is burnt on the outside and raw inside but it is also dangerous. To make sure this does not happen, check your barbecue is at the right temperature for cooking (the flames have died down, the coals are glowing and the tray is neither too close or too far away from the coals). Cut meat into small enough pieces to ensure that the centre is cooked sufficiently, and keep turning them so that all sides are cooked. Before serving, test the meat by cutting into the centre to see if it is done.

- When you are out and about on warm summer days remember that it is vital to make sure the children drink plenty of liquids to stay cool and hydrated. Children can become dehydrated long before adults because of their body size, and as they tend to run around a lot more this can lead to overheating. Your own sense of thirst is not the gauge to go by, so remember to ask them frequently if they would like a sip to drink. Don't let the increased need for 'potty stops' put you off. It is easiest to carry an individual bottle of water for each child to swig from as water is the best thirst quencher.

Parent Power

These are some useful resources for parents who would like to tackle the question of their child's school meals, and other issues.

- The Department for Education website, which gives information on catering standards and the dietary needs of special groups is www.dfes.gov.uk/schoollunches
- Contact the School Nutrition Action Group Campaign at www.healthedtrust.com for an excellent newsletter, general information and books such as *The Chips are Down*.
- The Health Education Unit for Key Stage 1 publications such as *It's Fun to Eat Vegetables* and *It's Fun to Eat Fruit* at healthed@birmingham.gov.uk or 0121 303 8200.
- A deputy head who is willing to discuss the changes made at his school is Steve Hatcher on stevehatcher@BTConnect.com, or 01423 885 814 or 07976 880 371. At St Aidan's High School in Harrogate they introduced a breakfast club and sixth form

café which were so successful that children from surrounding schools visit them. They brought in a professional chef who provides delicious school lunches, priced at school meal prices, which include home-made soups, traditional meals with vegetables, salads and fruit – and the kids are eating up.

- For a Food Dudes info pack aimed at schools so they can be more successful at getting children to eat more vegetables and fruit contact www.fooddudes.co.uk or the School of Psychology at the Bangor Food Research Unit on 01248 383 973.

- The Green Machine put vending machines in schools that offer healthy options, including, good quality muesli bars and yoghurts (subsidised by the food manufacturers to keep prices low). Contact David Berney at the Organic and Natural Food Company david@organicnatural.com or 020 8971 0055.

- The Kid's Cookery School in west London, 020 8992 8882 or www.thecookeryschool.co.uk, works with schools to educate children about cookery. Fifty per cent of places are assisted, the children are aged from three years up and they cater for special needs and ethnic minorities.

- The Parent's Jury is an action group which gathers a consensus of opinions from parents about food products aimed at children. They can be contacted c/o The Food Commission, 94 White Lion Street, London N1 9PF or at www.foodcomm.org.uk

- For inexpensive informative posters on additives in children's foods contact The Food Commission at the above address.

- For information on what to do about the provision of water in schools call 0117 960 3060 or visit www.wateriscoolinschools. co.uk

If you want to approach the head teacher at your child's school about nutritional and catering issues, it is as well to think a bit about the issues you may wish to discuss first:

– What is the existing food culture at the school?

- What are their probable awareness levels of the link between overall diet and health or behaviour?
- What are their current policies?
- Obviously, at meal times, they need to conform to certain nutrition standards (*see* School Catering, page 218), but do they allow canned drinks and soda drink dispensers, and can the children bring crisps and sweets to school?
- What is the tuckshop like?
- Do they link themselves to brands by allowing product advertising on school supplies? Do they encourage the collection of coupons by the children from certain manufacturers?

Once you have ascertained the answers to some of the above you can tailor your approach accordingly:

- What are the practicalities of making changes (in other words, what are the canteen facilities like)?
- Is fund raising likely to be necessary?
- Is it likely to be helpful to form a committee of like-minded parents who want to be involved?

Party Time

This is when good nutrition advice often falls apart. Assuming that parties only happen occasionally this really doesn't matter. However, children do enjoy a healthy party spread, and it will be cleared just as quickly as one with chicken nuggets, crisps, jelly and chocolate bars.

If this is your one-time-a-year cake bake you have the opportunity to make a delicious healthy cake with seasonal fruit, alternatively, a good quality chocolate cake always hits the mark. Even party bags don't have to go down the sweet and junk route – you can fill them up with non-sweet goodies such as marbles, hair bobbles, sticky note pads, pens and a slice of your lovely cake. Here are five party plans to break the typical junk-food party routine.

Finger Food for Little People

A table laid out with little pinwheel sandwiches, chicken 'meat-balls', pitted dates, carrot sticks, banana chips, and oat and chocolate flap-jacks.

Make Up Little Individual Party Boxes

Pack each box as you would a healthy lunchbox menu – *see* page 147 for ideas. Once they are through this lot it's time to wheel out the double chocolate cake!

Summer Theme Party

Have a picnic or barbecue – *see* page 187 for serving ideas. Spread out several tablecloths on the ground in the garden and let them at it!

Winter Theme Party

Make pumpkin heads with candles inside as decorations. With the scooped out flesh make a warming pumpkin soup. Follow with home-made hamburgers (*see* page 40) in a bun with relish, or vegeburgers or falafel with relish in a bun. Serve with baked potato skins crisped up with Parmesan (scoop out the flesh – use it in the soup – sprinkle on the cheese and put the skins back in the oven until the Parmesan is bubbling). Serve North-Pole icicles (lollies made out of banana and mango pulp and juice). If the children are old enough, put sparklers in the birthday cake to light up the dark winter evening.

Fancy Dress with a Themed Meal

Once you let your imagination rip you can come up with all sorts of ideas. A cowboy birthday party theme could include cowboy beans (black eyed beans or baked beans) with spareribs, vegetarian cow pie (make a vegetable pie and mock-up some cow-horns to stick out of it, though I don't know what Desperate Dan would make of the vegetables), lassoes made from liquorice ropes, stick cowboys and horses all over a home-made cake (mocked up to look like a rocky canyon using dried fruits).

See also Convenience Food – The Healthier Options, page 37.

Peanut and Other Allergies

Allergies are different to intolerances (*see* page 82). An allergy is an overactive immune response to things that do not normally trouble most people. They involve symptoms such as rashes, hives, eye or nasal irritation, asthma or swelling. The reaction is usually reasonably immediate upon exposure to the allergen (the substance to which the child is allergic). Common allergens include pollen, animal dander (hair and skin), house dust mites, washing powder and peanuts, though there are a host of other possibilities. Depending on the severity of the allergy, the problem can range from being a nuisance, to having a severe impact on daily life.

Allergies commonly run in families, and if so are referred to as 'atopic'. Such families have higher than average incidences of asthma, eczema, psoriasis, hay fever, allergic bowel problems, migraines and food allergies (such as peanut). If one of your children is allergic you need to be doubly cautious about your next child. Conversely, an allergy, such as peanut allergy, can come from nowhere. While the term 'allergy' is commonly applied to adverse food reactions, only 2 per cent of people are thought to have a true food allergy (as opposed to an intolerance).

Foods can be grouped into families which might not seem immediately obvious. For instance, potatoes, tomatoes, aubergines (eggplants), peppers and tobacco are all members of the deadly nightshade group. And while you might not think of them together in allergic terms, obviously chickens and eggs are related. This means that an allergy to one food can cross over to other related foods, or to foods that have similar compounds in them. This can make diagnosis of what is causing the problem difficult unless symptoms are very obvious. For instance, a silver birch (food family) allergy can involve allergic reactions to a combination of foods including fruit skins, carrots, apples, cherries and kiwis.

Possible Allergy Strategies

- Antihistamines. These are usually valid when the reaction is moderate and exposure can't be avoided. They are mostly used for problems such as hay fever or for moderate reactions to stings. For more information on hay fever, *see* page 79.
- Total avoidance of the allergen. This is particularly the case for foods that provoke a reaction, such as peanuts. The allergy is usually a lifetime problem.
- Adrenalin injections. These are used for severe reactions and can be life-saving for inadvertent exposure to serious allergens such as peanuts hidden in food or to insect stings. *See* Resources at the end of this section.
- Sometimes immunologists offer desensitisation injections but this is not usually valid for food allergies.
- In a significant number of instances, such as with hay fever, asthma, migraines and eczema (*see* relevant sections under Food as Medicine, page 71), you also have the possibility of reducing the overall 'load' placed on the immune system, as well as

bolstering the health of the immune system. These steps can have the effect of reducing the severity of the allergic reaction. It does not stop the 'trigger' from working, but reduces the 'trigger-happy' nature of the reaction. This is not, however, appropriate for severe allergies. *See also* Immune Boost, page 107.

Common Food Triggers

Peanuts are the food discussed here, however the information is equally appropriate for any serious food allergy. Most commonly these can include sesame seeds, tree nuts (such as pecans, walnuts, Brazils, almonds and others), egg whites, milk, citrus fruit, soya, shellfish, salmon or chicken. Kiwi fruit are becoming a common problem. Bee or wasp stings, certain drugs such as penicillin and latex from rubber gloves are also known to trigger allergies in sensitive children. In rare cases, closing up of the breathing tubes and anaphylactic shock can result, leading to death.

It is estimated that one in a hundred children have nut allergies. The most widespread 'nut' allergy is to peanuts. The peanut is not actually a nut but is a member of the legume family – the way peanuts line up in their pods reveals that they are in fact beans.

It is impossible to predict if a child is going to be allergic to a food, short of having an allergy test performed by a doctor. But as these tests are invasive, involving scratching the skin, they are not performed on a child unless it is to confirm a strong suspicion. Because peanut allergies are on the increase it is advised that nuts are not introduced until the age of three if they come from a family which tends to suffer allergies, including food allergies, asthma and eczema. If a reaction takes place, such as tingling in the mouth (*see* box below) take your child to the doctor immediately. There is a greatly increased trisk of anaphylaxis if your child is asthmatic, however not being an asthmatic does not rule out the occurence of a reaction.

But Nuts are a Good Food

Generally, nuts and peanuts are very good foods. They are excellent sources of protein, provide fibre and contain beneficial polyunsaturated fats. They make for convenient snacks and are packed with nutrients such as vitamin E, zinc and selenium. It is the fear of choking or allergy that means that health professionals are cautious about children eating them. Certainly choking is a very real risk, and for small children they need to be ground to avoid this as even chopped pieces can be inhaled. However, because of the concern over allergies, nuts are often not recommended, despite being highly nutritious. If your child is not allergic it may be a shame to avoid nuts totally, but you need to be aware and sensible. The main reason that those concerned with anaphylaxis to peanuts suggest that other nuts, which have a much lower allergic potential, are avoided is that food product labelling is often inaccurate and a label stating that it contains, say, walnuts, may actually include a proportion of much cheaper peanuts. If nuts are not likely to be a problem for your child I would have no qualms about introducing them cautiously, one by one and ground up, from an early age — say one year old (I gave them to my son at eight months). When introducing foods that have a potential to be allergic make sure that you are able to get to a doctor's surgery if necessary. In a way it is better to have a 'controlled experiment' rather than risk unexpected exposure in a restaurant or from packaged foods. Incidentally, it is the second exposure that causes an allergic reaction rather than the first, which is when the allergy-response is being 'primed' (though you may be unaware of the first exposure).

One of the problems with this type of allergy is that it is impossible to tell if reactions will be worse the next or subsequent times. Even if the reaction was mild initially, a full blown anaphylactic reaction can happen at later stages. For this reason you must carry prescribed medication at all times, even for those with mild allergies, and the school or older children must have their own supply.

Symptoms of Allergy Reaction

Serious symptoms could include

- Closing up of the throat
- Severe asthma
- A severe drop in blood pressure (weakness and floppiness)

Mild to moderate symptoms could include

- Itching or swelling in the mouth
- Hives anywhere on the body
- Flushing of the skin
- Nausea or vomiting

Symptoms usually happen very quickly within seconds or minutes, but sometimes also take up to a few hours.

Potential Sources of Peanut Proteins

There are various theories about why peanut allergies are on the increase. Peanuts and peanut oil (also called groundnut oil) are inexpensive ingredients and so find their way into a huge number of processed foods, such as biscuits, cakes, breakfast cereals, savoury foods, Asian foods, breads and confectionery, and this increased use might be partly to blame. It seems, however, that a reaction to refined peanut oil (found mainly in processed foods) is unlikely, but that unrefined peanut oil (mainly found in bottled oil and ethnic foods) has a higher risk of causing a reaction. It has also been suggested that babies can be sensitised (made allergic) in the womb if their mothers eat peanut-laced foods throughout their pregnancy, and peanut proteins are also found in breast milk if the mother eats peanuts. The widespread use of peanut oil in nappy creams, eczema creams and nipple creams has also come under scrutiny in recent years. In particular, there seems to be a risk from nappy and eczema creams being used on broken skin (in other words, used the way they are meant to be – on eczema).

Foods to Watch For in Nut Allergies

- Foods that can include nuts: cakes, pastries, desserts, chocolate, sweets, snacks, fruit yoghurts, biscuits, salads, salad dressings, dips, curries, chilli, stuffing, breakfast cereals.
- Some other foods to beware of include: pesto (pine nuts or walnuts), satay sauces (peanuts), marzipan (almonds), praline, nougat (almonds), halva (sesame seeds), hummus (sesame seeds), tahini (sesame seeds).
- Be aware that foods labelled as, say, containing almonds, may also contain peanuts (which are not labelled).

Food Labelling

Food manufacturers and supermarkets have finally become aware of the problems faced by peanut- and nut-allergic people. Since 1994, labelling has started to improve and many products are now labelled 'May Contain Nuts'. Manufacturers are also aware of the dangers of cross-contamination and some are opening segregated food production lines.

Different supermarkets have varying awareness and attitudes, but most have nutrition information lines that will tell you which products are suitable for those with allergies.

School Awareness

The situation in schools has also improved since the Department for Education published guidance and put in place means of training for local schools. But training staff in emergency procedures is problematic. The teaching unions have been cautious about their members being put in a difficult position and quite rightly insist that the schools take out indemnity insurance. The idea of administering life-saving injections can alarm them. It is often a good idea if they are initially contacted by a GP or health visitor who might know of other examples of children and schools affected by allergies and who can share their good practice.

The Family

Scary headlines can cause anxieties for allergic children and their families. Indeed the psychological impact can be great for some families, especially if they have had the trauma of seeing their child rushed to casualty. There is, inevitably, fear of the unknown and the need to send a child out into the world away from the protection of home can be very worrying. But the reality is that it is manageable and awareness is rising. Gradually anxiety eases over time as the parents and child gain control. It is important to educate, and not to smother, your child. Children can be very pragmatic about the situation and usually adapt well.

Ways to Avoid Trouble

- Always read food labels, and then still don't trust them.
- Research school menus and services in advance.
- Do similar research for proposed school trips.
- Talk to parents when your children are invited to tea or for birthday parties.
- Avoid high-risk places such as Asian restaurants who use lots of peanuts in their cuisine.
- Make sure waiters fully understand how important it is that no nuts should be used in the preparation of food – it is not enough to scrape nuts off the top of an ice-cream, for instance. This is true of other possible food allergies, for instance salmon may be stored next to other fish.
- Order simple dishes without sauces and batters.
- In highly allergic children even a greeting-kiss from a friend or relative who has eaten peanuts, or other allergenic food, could set off a reaction if it brushes their lips.
- Always carry an emergency adrenaline kit if prescribed.

Resources for Parents of Allergic Children

The most commonly used medication for severe allergies is the Epi-Pen®. This is easy to administer and does not have a protruding needle until after use. It looks like a pen, and contains a one-time shot of adrenaline (called epinephrine in the USA, hence the name). When activated, the needle is automatically triggered (blanks can be used to practice on, say, an orange). They are only available on prescription from your doctor and must be carried at all times in case of emergency. A minority of doctors are not as aware as they should be about the importance of prescribing them (I have heard complaints from parents about antihistamines being prescribed instead) so as a parent you need to be aware of their availability and use.

- Anaphylaxis Campaign Information Line, 01252 542 029 or www.anaphylaxis.org.uk
- Allergy UK is the leading medical charity and can be contacted on their helpline, 020 8303 8583, or at www.allergyuk.org
- British Society for Allergy and Clinical Immunology (020 8398 9240 or www.bsaci.soton.ac.uk) will supply GPs with a handbook of allergy clinics.
- The Department for Education guidelines for schools on nut allergies is available at www.dfee.gov.uk/schoollunches.annexa.htm
- Delyth Wakefield (01594 827 548 and www.peanutallergy awareness.com) gives advice to parents and serves the NHS direct line. She has also written a useful book *You Are Not Alone – Coping with Peanut Allergy*.
- Kidsaware (01480 869 244) provide a range of cool kids T-shirts, caps and stickers to warn of nut allergies, useful for school trips and outings.
- Kinnerton Confectionery (020 7284 9500 or www.kinnerton.com) produce completely nut-free confectionery, seasonal items (such

as Easter eggs) and a delicious birthday cake that is available from major supermarkets.

- Allergyfree Direct mail order foods are available at 01865 722003 or www.allergyfreedirect.co.uk
- The Healthy House (www.healthy-house.co.uk or 01453 752216) sells allergy-free bedding and other supplies.
- MedicAlert (0800 581420 or www.medicalert.co.uk) provides emergency medical identification tags.

Pester Power and Peer Pressure

Pester power and peer pressure are two of the cornerstones upon which the advertising and convenience food industries depend. But you CAN win through (most of the time) and you can even make these twin horrors work for you and not against you.

Ultimately, remember, that you have the right to say 'no'. Pester power only works if, as often as not, 'no' means 'maybe' and 'maybe' means 'yes'. Every child knows perfectly well, in these circumstances, that the odds are that they can wear you down, at least some of the time. Nobody says it is easy, least of all when you have a nagging, or even screaming, child at the checkout. As with a well known advertising campaign, remember you can 'Just Say No'. Be consistent about this. You may have to explain to your child the change in policy, and it may take a few days or even weeks before it sinks in that you are serious, but eventually it will work.

Reward good behaviour, but not bad. By buying stuff at the height of a full on 'pester' you reward bad behaviour. If your child knows that points can be earned towards a treat on a reward basis, he will (eventually) be motivated by this.

Interestingly, in the schools where major changes were made to lunches, school rules about what was allowed to be brought in lunchboxes, and policies on vending machines and tuck-shops, it was peer-pressure that won the day. Once a particular class made changes and saw benefits, it was those kids who influenced the classes above and below them to make and accept the changes. This is a perfect example of the positive benefits of peer pressure. You can use this to good advantage by inviting 'good eaters' over for tea, looking out for sports and pop figures who endorse some of the more positive products, and encouraging an interest in some of the younger TV chefs and their work.

Shopping Trips

Shopping with children can be like running an assault course. Pester power is turned on with full force. To help you get through the weekly food shop with your sanity intact here are a few ideas:

- In an ideal world shopping for food is a part of your child's education (I know this sounds idealistic!). The fresh food sections tend to be around the edge of most supermarkets. Make a point of cruising these and explaining to junior why you are doing this.
- For a change to your normal routine, it is great fun to check out a Farmers Market with children, and you can often get excellent quality and good prices (*see* Slow Food, page 221, for how to find addresses).
- Failing all else you could swap shopping child-minding sessions with a friend.
- The Co-Op Food Crimes report, which discusses many of the issues of pester power, is available at www.co-op.co.uk or by calling 0800 068 6727.

See also Advertising Whoppers, page 4.

Shopping Games

The object of games is to stop everyone getting on each others' nerves. Games keep children busy and happy and stop them nagging too much. You can plan a small non-junk food reward if they complete their task, say a magazine.

• With small children, give them a checklist of items to find as you go round together. It could be random items around the store or items with a theme, such as ten fresh items coloured pink and red (red pepper, meat, beetroot, strawberries, cut watermelon, prawns, etc.).
• To keep the older children guessing you could look for some weird and wonderful fruits and vegetables such as ugli, dragon fruit, star fruit, ackee, kiwano and others.
• Get your child to work out which is the healthiest yoghurt on offer and why.
• Ask your child to chose a recipe before you leave home and take the responsibility of collecting all the ingredients off the shelves.
• Give your child a shopping basket to collect items.
• Give older children a calculator and see if they can keep a running total of the bill as you go round.
• Also with older children ask them to 'pace out' the length of shelves of, say, colas and sodas and then compare them with the length of the fruit and vegetable shelves – there will be some surprises!

Projects and Activities

An awful lot of children, particularly urban ones, really can grow up having no idea where food comes from or how it grows. Yet if nobody tells them any different, this should come as no surprise. Encourage your child to learn about food with a variety of projects:

- Grow some food from seeds, even if you only have a plant pot or windowbox. By learning about the needs of plants a child learns that we need much the same things – nurturing, water, food, light, the right environment, and so on. And the quality of what we put into the food we grow also makes a difference in the quality of food we put into ourselves. Even in a very restricted space you could grow: cress, herbs, or sprouts from pulses (mung beans and lentils). Ideal for this are BioSnacky seeds (germinators are also available), available from Bioforce at www.bioforce.co.uk or by calling 0800 085 0803.

- If you have a little more space, such as a balcony, you could grow a tomato plant in a small growbag, or onions or cabbages in pots. Break up a garlic head into cloves and plant each clove. Eventually, by magic, these will each develop into a new garlic head.

- Other, very satisfying things to grow, which give the fast and/or spectacular results children appreciate include radishes (they grow in four weeks), sunflowers (which grow really tall – not a food, but fun), and marrows and pumpkins, which grow huge (you need space for these). With small children you will need to remind them to water the plants regularly and will probably have to help them do so.

- Make your own five-a-day chart. Cut out pictures of different fruits and vegetables from different magazines. Divide them into colour groups. The purple group might include red cabbage, aubergines, black grapes, blueberries, figs, kidney beans, and so on. Make a yellow group, and red, green and orange groups. Make collages and stick them to the fridge door. Then, using plain fridge magnets marked with your child's name, let them add a magnet to each chart when they eat a fruit or veg from that group. The ideal is one of each group each day. If you are feeling extravagant, you could buy enough magnets to last the whole week and see, together, how it pans out over a week. Children love keeping score.

- Another five-a-day idea is to get your child to draw around their hand on a sheet of paper. Five fingers, one for each portion. Colour the outline in pretty patterns. Stick the page on the fridge. As each portion is eaten, stick a fridge magnet on each finger. Start again the next day.

- Activities for outings (depending on whether you live in a town or can get to the countryside) could include:

  - A visit to a windmill to see how grain was processed in earlier days.
  - Asking a small bakers shop if you can visit to see how bread is made today.
  - A birthday party at a pizza restaurant where the children can make their own pizzas, starting with kneading the dough.
  - Going to a pick-your-own farm (see Seasonal Eating, page 220, to help deal with the 'glut').
  - Some farms do guided tours. Contact the Soil Association for information on this at www.soilassociation.org or call 0117 929 0661.
  - Gather seasonal wildfood in the countryside. Blackberries are a particular favourite, but you can also gather elderflowers in the spring to make cordial, and for older children mushroom hunting with a proper guide is great fun (some of the countryside associations will have details). Even (unsprayed) nettles make a delicious soup (take gloves!). With all wild food gathering, it is important to identify foods safely.

- At Hallowe'en, make a scooped out pumpkin lantern, but be sure to also make pumpkin soup together from the flesh.
- Start a family allotment to grow produce.

See also Learning About Food, page 138.

Questions

At the risk of stating the obvious, questions are the sign of a lively mind. Questions are not an irritation, they are to be welcomed (you may need to say this through gritted teeth to yourself a few times each day at the height of being driven mad by Why? What? and How? sessions). In particular, questions about food and health are to be encouraged. If you don't know the answer to a Why? question (such as, 'Why do I have to eat my vegetables?') find out and make it a learning experience for both of you. The answer, incidentally, is not 'Because I say so!'. Well, it may be the answer on occasions but it is much more useful to go to a book or the internet together and find out all the pros (there are almost no cons in answer to this question).

See also Young Helpers, page 277.

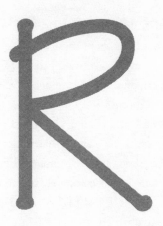

Restaurants

Thankfully the experience of eating out with children has improved dramatically, and gone are the days when children were not tolerated unless they were seen but not heard. Many restaurants understand the purchasing power of the kiddie-pound (or kiddie-euro or kiddie-dollar for that matter) and go out of their way to attract families with young children. Menus offering child-friendly choices, child portions and family-priced options are widely available.

Restaurants are not stupid and they offer what they know is popular. It has to be said, however, that most of the choices can be quite unimaginative and are restricted to what is perceived as 'children's food' with not much choice of different and interesting menus. And it is true that the average child will plump for burgers, chicken nuggets or sausages. But how many continental restaurants do you see with these options? I can't help but think that we lose something by not expanding our children's taste horizons. I would like to see more restaurants offering child-sized portions, at reasonable prices, of the adult menu, to give our children a better balance of nutrients and to avoid the pitfall of always eating the same types of foods. Starters are a good child-size; alternatively, if you have two or three kids in tow, you could get them to share an adult meal, divided up – if you are lucky enough to get them to agree on the choice!

As soon as your children are old enough to read, give them a menu to look through and discuss the choices with them. At earlier ages you can do the same while reading the menu to them.

Overall, my son and I both agree that trattatoria restaurants with a slight 1970s feel to them, run by Mama and Papa, are our favourite choice. Why? Because when compared to the corporate-style child friendliness, these people REALLY like children (and always seem to have a little treat up their sleeves when presented with a clean plate).

Salt Sellers

Salt is added to foods because it works so well as a flavour enhancer and makes all sorts of less appealing dishes more desirable. For instance, it makes fatty foods taste less greasy. One of the taste sensations on the tongue is salt, along with sweet, sour, bitter and umami. Umami is the flavour that is typical of Japanese food and in Western processed foods it is represented by the heavy use of MSG (monosodium glutamate), which is a major source of added sodium.

Salt has a bad name because we tend to get too much of it on a Western diet, but actually the sodium it contains is a vital mineral. During our evolution, sodium was relatively hard to come by and so our bodies developed a means of retaining this essential mineral. We became so good at this that, now we find ourselves living in a time of salty processed foods, we are typically overloaded with sodium. This contributes to high blood pressure, which in turn is linked to heart disease and stroke. High levels also contribute to water retention and to calcium loss from bones.

Making Sense of Sodium/ Salt

In order to make sense of the sodium levels declared on food packaging you need to convert the sodium figure per portion or per 100g into the equivalent amount of salt. Sodium makes up 40 per cent of table salt or salt in food products – the remaining 60% is chloride and salt is called sodium chloride. To get the salt figure, multiply the sodium figure given by 2.5. Therefore:

0.5 g sodium	=	1.25 g salt
1.0 g sodium	=	2.5 g salt
2.0 g sodium	=	5 g salt

It also helps to know that:

3 g of salt	=	1 level teaspoon

The above is a slight oversimplification because some products give the total added sodium (ignoring natural sodium) and some give the total sodium content (natural salt present in the food plus the added sodium). Monosodium glutamate (E621) and bicarbonate (baking soda) may be ignored in the sodium count. MSG can be disguised on the ingredients listing as: hydrolysed protein, natural flavouring, seasoning, spices, vegetable bouillon and plant protein extract.

Sea salt is also made up of sodium chloride but also contains other minerals such as magnesium, potassium and iodine. This means that the sodium in sea salt is about two-thirds of the equivalent amount of table salt.

Children are consuming on an average, twice, and often three times, the salt they should. Babies should have no salt added to their food at all. Children can have some salt, but not as much as adults. The majority of salt that children consume comes from packaged foods, though salt added to cooking, and table salt contribute as well.

Recommended Daily Sodium/Salt Intakes

	Sodium	Salt	Maximum Salt	Typical Intake
1–3 years	0.5 g	1.25 g	2 g	1.4 g
4–6 years	0.7 g	1.75 g	3 g	5.0 g
7–10 years	1.2 g	3.0 g	5 g*	5.8 g
11–18 years	1.6 g	4.0 g	5 g	6.5 g

*Some authorities believe the 7–10 years figure would be better set at 3–4 g.

Salt appears in the funniest (or unfunniest, depending on how you look at it) places. For instance, you might think that cutting out crisps would be a good place to start to reduce salt intake. And yet an equivalent amount of cornflakes has a lot more salt than most crisps. Because of the amount eaten, staples such as bread make up a significant part of intake, and even though salt levels in bread have recently been reduced we still get far too much. Foods such as sausages, cheese and tinned pasta take levels sky-high. And, believe it or not, products such as spaghetti hoops, marketed specifically at children with cartoon characters, are often higher than their equivalent 'adult' products. Takeaway and convenience foods, and smoked and preserved foods are other familiar sources. It is generally unnecessary to add salt to the cooking water of rice or pasta.

By eating a can of pasta shapes, some sausages and Marmite sandwiches, a child easily exceeds the maximum recommended level. The most effective way to cut back is to switch from regular use of packaged foods to making more meals from scratch where you can control the amount of salt used.

It is worth thinking about the difference that cooking with unprocessed ingredients can make to sodium intake – look at these comparable foods, per 100 g:

frozen peas	0.003 g	canned processed peas	0.25 g
unsalted butter	0.01 g	salted butter	0.75 g
beef, lean	0.06 g	beefburger	0.60 g
tomato purée	0.02 g	ketchup	1.12 g
pork, lean	0.07 g	sausages	0.76 g
haddock, fresh	1.20 g	haddock, smoked	12.20 g
pasta, cooked	0.05 g	pasta shapes, tinned	0.40 g

A taste for salt can be curbed over time by gradually reducing dependency on salt and salty foods. Using chopped herbs and ground spices in your cooking instead of salt is a great way to 'divert' taste interest elsewhere. You could experiment with a sprinkle of lemon, parsley, chives, coriander, cumin, tarragon and others. Developing a taste for less salty foods is a gift for a child.

For more information about salt contact CASH (Consensus on Salt and Health) at www.hyp.ac.uk/cash or call 020 8725 2409.

Sodium / Salt Content of Typical Portions of Food

	Sodium	Salt
bacon (25 g – 2 rashers)	0.37 g	0.92 g
baked beans (200 g)	1.06 g	2.65 g
bread, 1 medium slice (35 g)	0.18 g	0.45 g
burger, takeaway kid's meal with bun, small fries and small cola	1.32 g	3.3 g
butter, salted, 10 g (2 tsp – av. 1 slice bread)	0.07 g	0.18 g
cheese, yellow 50 g	0.35 g	0.87 g
chicken nuggets (50 g)	0.5 g	1.25 g
convenience lunchbox with crackers, ham and cheese	1.1 g	2.75 g
cornflakes, 35 g serving	0.33 g	0.82 g
crisps (35 g – 1 small pkt)	0.2 g	0.5 g
egg (1)	0.14 g	0.35 g
fish fingers (3 – 100 g)	0.3 g	0.75 g
ketchup, 1 level tsp (5 g)	0.06 g	0.15 g
Marmite/Bovril, 1 level tsp (5 g)	0.25 g	0.62 g
noodle snack (89 g)	1.8 g	4.5 g
pasta shapes, tin (205 g)	0.8 g	2.0 g
pizza, slice (200 g)	1.2 g	3.0 g
sausages (50 g)	0.38 g	0.95 g
tomato soup, canned (100 g)	0.45 g	1.12 g

School Catering

At last, after 20 years of a free-for-all, UK schools now have nutritional standards they must stick to for children's meals. When compulsory standards were scrapped in the 1980s, chips, pizza and fizzy drinks began to appear on the menu, and children could easily go through a day without eating a 'square meal'. Now the standards have decreed that schools move away from a 'chips with everything' approach.

Food might be prepared in different ways, depending on the size of the school and facilities available. Some have dedicated 'dinner ladies' (95 per cent of them are women) who prepare, cook and serve the meals. For other schools, the meals are cooked at a central location and brought in, airline style, to be heated up. All schools should provide a daily vegetarian option. If a school is in an area with a majority of children coming from a particular ethnic group then this will be catered for, for example by providing Kosher options, or Halal meat, or making sure that the vegetarian option fits the bill. The school may also specify that some nut-free or coeliac (gluten-free) meals be provided.

The main problem with the new standards are that they do not set guidelines for the *quality of the ingredients* used. At around 40p per head, the caterers have to be magicians to squeeze good value out of a meal and inevitably that means that the quality of the ingredients is going to be poor. The standard of meals in many schools is so low that many children prefer to bring in packed lunches. Additionally, there are usually still no overall counts of salt and fat levels in the meals and so there is much room for improvement. Any moves to improve this are sporadic and unconnected and completely dependent on the efforts of the individual school, of which there are some good examples showing that it can be done. We also know that better ingredients for school meals are possible on a national basis because the Italians have very successfully legislated on this matter.

Minimum UK Nutritional Standards

Nursery Schools

Must provide foods for lunch from each of the following groups each day:

A) Fruits and Vegetables, whether fresh, frozen, canned, dried or juices.
B) Starchy foods such as bread, chapatis, pasta, noodles, rice, potatoes, sweet potatoes, yams, millet and cornmeal.
C) Meat, fish or vegetarian sources of protein such as eggs, nuts, pulses and beans (excludes dairy).
D) Milk and dairy foods, such as cheese, yoghurt, custard, milk-shakes (but not butter or cream).

Primary Schools

Must provide from each of the above groups as well but have more stringent specifications:

A) Fruit (fresh or tinned) must be available daily.
A vegetable must also be provided daily (excludes potatoes, yams, and sweet potatoes).
Fruit-based desserts, such as apple pie or fool, must be available at least twice a week.
B) Fats or oils must not be used in cooking starchy foods more than three times a week (i.e. offer baked potatoes instead of chips).
C) Fish must be available at least once a week (could include fish fingers or tinned fish).
Red meat must be available at least twice a week.
Protein can also include some foods from the dairy group, such as cheese and yoghurt.

Typical school lunch – 1980s

At the time when regulations were scrapped, the chances are that a 'square meal' was eaten even if it now looks a little old-fashioned.

- Liver and bacon or steak and kidney pie
- Mashed potato or boiled potatoes
- Cabbage or carrots and peas
- Steamed sponge and custard or semolina and jam
- Tap water

Typical school lunch – 1990s

When things had really gone downhill the foods offered were much higher in fat, salt and sugar and the salad bar was often left untouched.

- Hamburger or sausages
- Chips
- Salad bar
- Fruit yoghurt or jelly and cream
- Fizzy drinks or diluted fruit squash

Typical school lunch – 21st century

Now standards have been introduced, things have improved.

- Pasta tuna bake or ovenbaked chicken grill
- Potato wedges or creamed potatoes
- Seasonal vegetables or salad
- Apple and raspberry sponge or fruit salad and custard
- Water, milk or whole fruit juice

Seasonal Eating

Encouraging children to be aware of the seasonality of food is a good thing. With the wide availability of produce at all times, it is easy to forget that foods have natural growing seasons. Yet it can be great fun, and rewarding, to look forward to the advent of summer when local strawberries, baby broad beans and asparagus first appear in the shops, or to autumn and winter when pumpkins and chestnuts are available. Taking advantage of the bounty seasons adds a whole new dimension to enjoying and learning about food.

Of course we know that these days we can get hold of tomatoes year round, apples are shipped in from the Antipodes and strawberries are not just a summer commodity. But there are definite drawbacks to this. Fruits which have been shipped long distances often do not taste nearly as good as the same produce eaten in their country of origin. This is usually because they have been picked unripe and then ripened in transit. Fruit is much tastier, and nutrient rich, if it is tree-ripened. Seasonal ingredients also tend to go together – for instance, apple and blackberry, salmon and asparagus or pheasant and cranberry.

When berries such as blueberries and redcurrants are cheap, that is the time to buy and freeze – this way you can get a little bit of summer in the colder months. Not only is cooking from a glut economic but it can also stretch your culinary expertise. Give your child the job of looking up in your cookery books all the different ways, for instance, you can cook cabbage or apples and decide between you which dishes sound the nicest. You can take full advantage of inexpensive produce by freezing the dishes you make. Even if you do something as simple as making stewed plums when they are in season, it can be immensely satisfying, particularly later when they can be brought out and turned into a crumble or just served with Greek yoghurt or ice cream for a nutritious and delicious pudding.

Slow Food

Increasingly, we live in a fast-food world. In response to this, and in an attempt to restore the value of food and mealtimes as a funda-mental core of family life, the Slow Food movement was started in Italy in 1989. Slow Food really took off and now is represented all over the world. We all know that eating as a family and enjoying food together is important socially and nutritionally, but changing entrenched habits takes some thought. Here is how to get the slow food habit with your family:

- Introduce your children to real food as soon as they can eat to develop a relationship with food via the senses. With older chil-dren cook with them, take them to farms, grow food, have herbs or tomato plants in pots, visit a baker.
- Treat meal preparation as a hobby to be enjoyed instead of a chore to be endured. Share this hobby with your children.
- Enjoy eating with friends and family. Make it a relaxed social affair and enjoy conversation. Your children will learn a lot from this.
- Audit how many fast-food/convenience meals your family eats each week and aim to prepare fresh food in future for at least half of these.
- Shop at farmers' markets or shops supplying local produce. For a list of locally sourced foods look at www.farmersmarkets.net, www.localfood.org.uk, and www.thesoilassociation.org
- Cook with seasonal produce (*see* page 220).
- Some slow food recipes actually take very little time to prepare, just longer to cook – for example stuffed jacket potatoes, fresh vegetable and bean soups, sauce for pasta or rice, roast lemon chicken, baked fish with vegetable kebabs.
- Make use of your freezer. *See* Busy Parents, page 30, for ideas.

- Make your next holiday a cooking holiday in your own country or abroad, to learn about real food.
- Find out about children's cookery courses near you. Near London contact the Kids' Cookery School at www.thekidscookery school.co.uk or call 020 8992 8882. They also run courses for schools.
- Check out www.slowfood.com

Store Cupboard Standbys

Being able to whisk up a healthy meal from thin air is a talent not many of us have. In order to have healthy and delicious options always to hand when faced with a fast approaching teatime, it helps to have a groaning cupboard full of things you can throw together pretty quickly. This way you are less likely to fall back on those old favourites, such as the dastardly chicken nugget (for reasons why the chicken nugget is so dastardly, *see* page 39).

- Canned and bottled foods that are handy in a crisis include: tomatoes, tomato purée, beans of all sorts (flageolet, kidney, black eyed, navy, and – yes – even baked), lentils, sardines, mackerel, anchovies, tuna, salmon, chestnut purée, coconut milk, olives, sun-dried tomatoes, peppers in olive oil, pesto sauce, chutneys. I much prefer fresh fruit but one or two cans of fruit in natural juices and not in syrup might be handy, especially dark berries, which mix well with stewed apple and yoghurt.
- Dried and vacuum-packed foods: tortilla wraps, dried mush-rooms, crackers, garlic paste, coconut or almond flakes, dried fruit, popcorn, pasta (different grains), rice, porridge, couscous, millet flakes, noodles, pasta shapes.

- Packets of fresh nuts and seeds. Make sure they are fresh when you buy them and store them, unopened, in the fridge if you are keeping them for any length of time.
- Keep a good stock of dried herbs and spices to add pep to dishes. Left over wine is good for sauces and stocks and as the alcohol cooks off it is fine for children.
- Freezer compartment. Contrary to popular belief, frozen vegetables are as good as fresh – they have often been picked at their peak and so are nutritionally full of goodness. Good options include: peas, green beans, carrots, spinach, sweetcorn. Other foods that keep well in the freezer include fresh soups, prawns, hummus, pitta breads, grated hard cheeses, ready-rolled pastry.
- Some fresh foods last a fair amount of time if they are kept cool. Make sure you have: onions, garlic, potatoes, lemons, oranges or other citrus fruit, corn on the cob and eggs.

Emergency Meals

What could you make with these store cupboard standbys, with relative ease?:

- Lentil, tomato and onion soup – a main meal
- Tortilla wrap with beans, sun-dried tomato and anchovy
- Fishy pasta sauce with tuna, tomato, onion and peas
- Vegetable coconut curry
- Baked stuffed potato with hummus
- Wild mushroom risotto
- Spinach and cheese omelette
- Wholemeal pitta pizzas – use pittas as an instant pizza base
- Dark berry millet porridge
- Vegetables pastries with peanut and mango chutney dipping sauce

Sugar

All children love sugar, but sugar (or at least too much of it) doesn't love them. A smidgen of sugar does no harm, and as a flavour enhancer can be used to encourage a child to eat all sorts of good foods. For instance, a modest spoonful of sugar on a baked apple or bowl of porridge is, on balance, a good thing (even if nutrient-rich raisins or mashed banana might be a better option). But the problems with too much sugar in the diet include:

- High sugar snacks and drinks blunt children's appetites at meal times.
- Sugar has no accompanying nutrients. The 'empty calories' are automatically displacing other nutrient-rich ingredients in the diet.
- Frequent consumption encourages tooth decay.
- Too much sugar on a regular basis can encourage poor blood-sugar handling (see Energy, page 59).
- Excess sugar is converted into fat in the blood very quickly. These triglycerides are then stored as body fat. If a child is inactive this increases the chances of excess weight.
- Becoming used to excessively sweet foods blunts the taste for fresh foods, which are better sources of nutrients.
- As with salt (see page 213), sugar is found most frequently in processed foods, which usually means that the sugar is also disguising high fat levels and, often, food additives and colourings.

How Much is Too Much Sugar?

One hundred years ago sugar was a luxury and average intake was 1 teaspoon a day. Compare this with the current UK average of 20 teaspoons daily (and the US average of 28 teaspoons daily) and you begin to see where we are going wrong. A lot of this comes from confectionery, but most comes from packaged, processed foods. Refined sugar (either the white or brown stuff) is not necessary in the diet. The problem with many products is that you just don't know how much is in them.

- Remember that the amount of sugar per 100 g of product is the same as saying per cent. So if there is 19 g sugar per 100 g it is also 19% sugar, or, to put it another way, nearly one-fifth sugar, which is a lot. A recent government report states that over 10 per cent sugar in the diet should be viewed as excessive.

- In visual terms, 10 g of sugar is 2 teaspoons. Many children's cereals are, for instance, up to 50 g sugar per 100 g product. If a typical serving is 40 g of product, then 20 g is pure sugar – or 4 teaspoons.

- Ingredients are listed in order of quantity, so if sugar appears at the top of the list then this is a clue. Other names for sugar include glucose, glucose syrup, syrup, honey, fructose and dextrose. Maltodextrine is a partially hydrolysed (broken down) starchy filler which is metabolised into sugar in the blood very quickly.

- To imagine how much of an impact sugary foods have it helps to know that an adult has 2–3 teaspoons of sugar in the blood at any one time. This is blood sugar available for immediate energy needs and the level is carefully regulated by the body so it gets neither too high (which would indicate diabetes) or too low (which would lead to fainting fits, or low blood sugar). Children will have relatively less than this, depending on their size, so let's say 1 teaspoon's-worth in a child's bloodstream. The average chocolate bar contains around 8 teaspoons of sugar, and a can of cola has around 4 teaspoons in it. So it is easy to see how these can impact on a child's blood sugar balance. The excess sugar leads to feeling overalert and 'speedy' and in order to stop it causing metabolic problems the body has to store it, as a matter of urgency, as fat. The mechanism can get trigger happy with too much insulin produced to clear blood sugar into fat stores. This leads to low blood sugar. The brain is semi-starved of fuel and the body does not function properly, leading to fatigue, irritability, poor concentration, spaciness and nerv-ousness – in other words a child who is a nightmare to deal with. This low blood sugar creates cravings for more sugar and so the cycle is perpetuated.

How Can You Tempt Your Child Away From Too Much Sugar?

It is not necessary, or practical, to ban sugar completely – just get it into context. It is an occasional choice, not a meal in its own right! The best way to eat sugar is with other foods which are high in fibre. This slows down the rate of digestion and consequently its absorp-tion into the blood. Therefore some jam on wholemeal bread or some sugar in an oat flapjack or a fruit cobbler is better than a sweet or even, from a blood sugar point of view, a glass of undiluted fruit juice.

- Offer non-sugary snacks such as hummus on a cracker, a small sandwich, a few vegetables with avocado dip or cream cheese. *See* Munchies, page 169, for ideas.
- Offer water or a little milk as drinks. Restrict juices to meal times and favour fresh juices, partially diluted with water.
- Get into the habit of nearly always offering juicy chunks of fruit for dessert after meals. Watermelon, crispy apples, kiwi, plums and ripe pears all satisfy a sweet tooth.
- Offer better alternatives to over-sweetened foods. For instance, mash a banana or other sweet fruit into Greek yoghurt as an alternative to pre-sweetened yoghurts or desserts.

- Encourage a taste for good quality chocolate with a high cocoa content. Most commercially available chocolate has 10 per cent cocoa solids, but better choices have 30–60 per cent. Of course, the higher cocoa content will also mean caffeine, so avoid late at night and spread the effect of the treat by making it part of a bigger treat (say strawberries dipped in chocolate). Chocolate is not as bad for teeth as other sweets are.
- Make delicious healthy smoothies and shakes by adding sweet fruit and berries to milk, soya or rice milk.
- Whiz up berries, mango or kiwi in a blender to make a colourful sauce to accompany desserts.
- Chopped up, nutrient-rich, fruit or dried fruit added to cereals are better than sugary versions.
- If your child already has a sweet tooth you may need to be patient. For instance, slowly reduce the amount of cordial in his drinks over time until a negligible amount, or none, is used and he enjoys the taste of water.

See also Sweeteners, below, and Desserts, page 42.

Sweeteners

In an effort to give their children healthier, low-sugar options, many parents offer, knowingly or unknowingly, foods which are laced with artificial sweetners. The reasoning can be that artificial sweeteners are not detrimental to dental health, do not affect blood sugar levels and are low in calories – all of which are true. They may also be used by diabetic children.

Artificial sweeteners are in a wide range of foods consumed by children – even though, by law, they are not meant to be. Manufacturers claim that the foods are not specifically aimed at children, though this is patently nonsense when they carry cartoon characters. Foods which commonly contain added artificial sweeteners include fizzy drinks, juice drinks, squashes (they are in both normal and diet versions of most drinks), ice lollies, some yoghurts, reduced-sugar desserts, reduced-sugar and standard baked beans, sauces such as ketchup and salad cream, some flavoured crisps and sugar-free chewing gum. They are also found in chewable vitamin supplements and medicines.

What the Labels Mean

Sugar free — Free of natural sugars, but could well (or is likely to) contain artificial sweeteners (check the label).

Low sugar — Contains less than 5 g sugar per 100 g of product, but could also contain artificial sweeteners (check the label).

No added sugar — No natural sugars added but may contain honey, concentrated fruit juice or artificial sweeteners (check the label).

Because these chemically derived compounds are 200–300 times as sweet as sugar only a small amount is needed. But the small amounts build up with regular consumption and they encourage a sweet tooth. Additionally, because foods and drinks with sweeteners are lower in calories they have the effect of overriding the 'fullness' feedback mechanism that is triggered by higher calorie content foods. This can encourage diet food consumers to actually eat more. In any case, diet foods are simply not appropriate for children as they have lower nutrient contents. Concerns surrounding artificial sweeteners include dizziness, bloating, hyperactivity and cancers.

The acceptable daily intakes (ADI) of the various sweeteners can easily be overstepped by a child consuming everyday foods. A sweetened yoghurt, a savoury snack, an ice lolly or dessert and four sweetened juice drinks will do it. There are different ADIs for different sweeteners making it difficult to keep a check.

Labelling laws are not always adhered to by manufacturers, in whose interest it is to be vague. Although manufacturers are legally required to list the use of sweeteners on the main label, up to 50 per cent don't do so and it is hidden in the small print at the back. The penalties are not sufficient to make them toe the line and be clear about what they contain. Even those that do not claim to be low-sugar or artificially sweetened often contain sweeteners. This is likely to be a price issue – artificial sweeteners cost a lot less than sugar, making it economically attractive to replace sugar with sweeteners. Products labelled as low-fat usually have very high sugar levels to compensate taste-wise and are likely to contain artificial sweeteners.

If you want to avoid sweeteners you just need to look for products that do not contain them. You will have to accept that if your child is to eat some sweet foods they will get a certain amount of sugar, but keep their taste for sweet foods curbed by giving them natural sources of sweetness, such as fruits, and limiting the worst sweet foods.

The Main Sweeteners and Possible Problems

Aspartame/NutraSweet (E951) This is made from two amino acids (protein building blocks) and is broken down 'naturally' in the body. Children diagnosed with phenylketonuria must avoid it (products carry a warning). This is a condition where the body is unable to break down phenylalanine, leading to convulsions. Commonly reported side effects of aspartame are headaches and migraines, dizziness and blurred vision. Research shows that aspartame worsens brainwave readings in children with epilepsy. Aspartame separates into methanol (wood alcohol), formaldehyde, aspartic acid and phenylalanine in the body. Links with brain cancer are being investigated.

Acesulfame K (E950) This is linked to cancer in animals.

Saccharine (E954) Products containing saccharine in the USA must carry a cancer health warning. It may also adversely affect hyperactivity.

Cyclamate (E952) Originally banned, this sweetener is currently available, though there are renewed proposals in Europe to ban it. One can of cyclamate sweetened drink would meet the ADI for a toddler. Links between cyclamate and testicular cancer are being investigated.

Sorbitol (E420) This is a naturally occurring indigestible sugar. Along with xylitol (below) this is called a bulk sweetener rather than an intense artificial sweetener. Sorbitol is mainly used to sweeten diabetic foods such as jams and sugar. Because of its indigestibility it can cause bloating and diarrhoea when eaten in large quantities.

Xylitol (E967) This is another naturally occurring indigestible sugar with many of the same qualities as sorbitol. On a positive note, it is used in chewing gum as it has been shown to dramatically reduce decay-causing bacteria in the mouth (see Toothy Issues, page 236).

Tens and Teens

Despite looking almost like adults, teenagers have much the same nutritional needs as younger children – they are still growing at a furious pace and they still need to eat a nutrient-rich diet. Added to this, their bodies are also changing as they head towards, and go through puberty. Top this up with participation in sports, or exam pressures, or some crash dieting, and it easy to see how teenagers can become run down. Unfortunately, this is also the time when they are most likely to become, temporarily, lost causes on the health and nutrition front. But if you have managed to do some groundwork with a varied diet beforehand, the chances are that they will ride out this time and eventually return to the fold, though by this time you may have already have had a nervous breakdown.

It is increasingly common for children to experience early puberty – the average age has been steadily dropping over the last century from around 14 to 11, and in a significant minority it can be as early as eight years old, which can confuse any child. In any event, this age group are prone to being confused. Modern pressures can be immense in terms of expectations of growing into adulthood, confusion about sexuality, cigarettes, alcohol or drugs and coping with peer pressures.

It used to be thought that teenagers were just confused with so much learning to do about life. But it might be some consolation for the harassed and despairing parent to find out that there is also a neurological basis for their irrational and difficult behaviour. There is a significant growth spurt in the brain and a reorganisation of nerve connections. Their brains are literally being 'remodelled'. The activity in the brain is making it difficult for them to process basic information and to recognise other people's emotions. So their behavioural changes are likely to be rooted in very real physical changes. Put another way, it isn't their fault (I realise this is being very generous, but might make the lack of comprehension that a parent feels a little easier to deal with). In one interesting study, the ability to identify with other people's emotions dropped by 20 per cent in 11 year olds and then improved slightly each year thereafter, only returning to normal at age 18. I don't wish to imply that all teenagers are awful – I can think of some lovely teens I have known – but there are some stereotypical situations which are borne out by statistics (teenage eating disorders, depression, pregnancy, etc.). There is no one pat 'ideal' way to deal with awkward teenagers, but here are some suggestions anyway:

- If their diet is truly ghastly at least persuade your teen to down a daily vitamin and mineral supplement. This could be particularly important in the couple of months leading up to exam times.
- Appeal to your child on health terms that are meaningful to them – sports interest, clearing up a skin problem, having enough energy to party.
- Keep up an interest in food preparation if possible, using positive role models, such as some of the TV chefs.
- Whatever you do don't overdo the health angle or nag, you will only be playing to type.

- If you despair at their lack of breakfast-eating and fast-food or grazing habits, remember that just one good solid meal a day can make all the difference in health, ability to concentrate, physical and emotional wellbeing. Concentrate on this, rather than worrying about all the times you can't control.

- If your child has taken to vegetarianism, which is particularly common amongst young teenage girls, make sure they have information about healthy vegetarianism. There is no doubt that a vegetarian diet can be just as healthy as an omnivorous one (or even healthier) as long as educated choices are made. It is not enough just to drop meat; it is important to include choices which are protein, zinc and iron rich to compensate. *See* Vegetarians and Vegans, page 246.

- It is important to realise that a large number of young girls can become anaemic when they start menstruating. If they have low iron stores to start off with, the blood loss can tip them into anaemia. This can impact upon energy levels and concentration. If your child seems pale and listless ask your doctor to check for serum ferritin levels. *See* page 264 for ways to boost iron from the diet. If necessary, give her an iron supplement (but do not do this without checking for anaemia first). Spatone+, a liquid, is more gentle than most supplements and can avoid side effects such as constipation – find out more at www.spatone.com or call 0800 7311 740. Another supplement is Ferrogreen, available by calling 08450 606070.

- As with any teenage issue, it is important to communicate clearly and calmly to avoid it spiralling into a ghastly argument. Listen to what your child has to say and his reasons, no matter how different to your beliefs, to understand the situation better. Focus on the positive – find anything you can that is good and explore and expand on this. Your child is growing into an independent being and you can no longer lay down the law, but need to reason. Obviously, you do have the right to make house rules, but as they are more independent you may just force them into lying and being more out of control when out of sight. It's best to talk straight and be accommodating – up to a point.

- It can be helpful to involve another person who your child trusts, such as a relative or close friend.

See also Disordered Eating, page 49.

Toddlers and Food Independence

As children grow it is natural that, bit by bit, they become more independent from their parents. It is what we all want for our children, for them to become capable and content independent people. But the road to this destination is, often, a rocky one (*see* Tens and Teens, page 232).

One of the first holds that a child has over their parent, after crying and smiling and before toilet training, is the start of independence with food. From the age of about one, children can wield a spoon and before that use their fingers to pick up tid-bits, even if more food ends up on the floor instead of in their mouths. Luckily, at about this time, their calorie needs also take a bit of a dive.

The next stage is the ability to refuse food. Short of force-feeding (which is never desirable!) there is not much you can do to get something into a toddler who is refusing food. It is important to realise that by this point toddlers are cottoning-on fast to the idea that they can manipulate their parent(s) by eating or refusing foods. Rise to this situation emotionally at your peril. It is important to always remain calm – or at least most of the time, you are not a saint. Assuming you have offered your child a meal that should be acceptable, at the end of the meal, say half-an-hour from starting, put the food away. Do not offer alternatives, no matter how worried you are, and wait until the next meal time or scheduled snack. Hunger will take over at the next meal, or the one after that. What this is all about is setting boundaries. If you become a slave to offering any food, no matter what, your child is setting the boundaries. If you calmly set the pattern then it is you that is setting the boundaries.

Toddlers also go through phases of refusing foods that they have previously eaten quite happily. Again, this is to do with testing the situation and flexing their independence. Keep offering the food periodically over time and there is every likelihood it will be taken up again.

Praise any good choices they make, no matter how small, to help reinforce their new positive habits.

The next stage in independence is when your small child starts school. At this time they, increasingly, will be able to make their own choices about what they eat. You cannot be with your child all the time, so the key issue here is the groundwork you have done to promote an interest in a wide variety of foods, tastes and flavours, and knowledge about food and food preparation, no matter how basic.

Once your toddler is away from home more often, at playschool or at friends' houses, they will inevitably be faced with different food choices. Children often do not have a conflict about this and they learn very quickly that there can be one set of rules for the home and other options when away from home. They may eat food that you are not totally thrilled about when away from home, but it doesn't have to be a problem as most children will settle back into home eating patterns without any trouble at all.

See also Choice, page 35, and Faddy Eating, page 63.

Toothy Issues

There are three main causes of preventable dental problems in children – gum disease, tooth decay and dental erosion. Good dental hygiene (brushing and flossing) and regular visits to the dentist, and ideally the hygienist, are obviously essential. But the effect of diet on dental health is the other primary tool for keeping a full set of healthy teeth from childhood.

Nutrients for Healthy Teeth and Gums

The nutrients needed for healthy teeth are the same as for bones. Eating calcium- and magnesium-rich foods is important (*see* Milk and Dairy, page162). Ensuring that your child gets out of doors means that he will get adequate vitamin D, the sunshine vitamin that we make in our skin on exposure to sunlight, to help bones and teeth to assimilate calcium. Regular brushing will help to keep gums firm and healthy, but so will a vitamin C-rich diet. One of the first signs of scurvy, or vitamin C deficiency, is soft, pulpy and bleeding gums because vitamin C is needed to build the collagen that keeps gums strong. Make sure your child gets five portions of fruit and vegetables daily, of which at least one should ideally be vitamin C-rich, for example citrus, kiwi, strawberries, blackcurrants, cabbage or broccoli.

Tooth Decay

You are probably already aware of the causes of tooth decay – bacteria in dental plaque interacts with sugars from food producing localised acid that leads to decay, or caries, which in turn makes fillings necessary. Sugar and other carbohydrates act as food for mouth bacteria. What is important is the *frequency* of intake of sugar and carbohydrates. From a tooth decay point of view it is best to eat any sugary snacks with a meal rather than on their own, which increases the number of exposures. A better snack would be a small cube of cheese with some vegetable sticks (though telling this to the average child may not gain favour). Chocolate is actually not as cariogenic – tooth decay forming – as other sweets because the cocoa butter it contains coats and protects teeth somewhat.

Believe it or not it is actually best to brush teeth before breakfast (or even better would be both before and after). The reason for this is that bacteria have had a chance to build up overnight and acids begin to form within *seconds* of exposure to any sugars in the breakfast meal. It also will not please many parents to know that chewing gum with xylitol in it, an indigestible sugar, is a potent aid for protecting teeth. Xylitol stops bacteria adhering to the tooth surface and so reduces damage significantly. Finally, a very useful tool in preserving teeth against the need for fillings is to ask your dentist to coat the surface of permanent molar teeth with a fissure sealant that acts as a barrier against bacteria.

Tooth Erosion

This is a different problem to tooth decay and affects large numbers of children, though awareness of this is fairly low. Erosion is caused by the direct impact of acidic foods and drinks on the entire tooth enamel, causing it to soften and lose minerals, eventually eroding the whole surface of the tooth. This ultimately results in the soft under-layer, the dentine, being exposed. Signs of tooth erosion are a 'glassiness' of the teeth, sensitivity to cold, heat and sweetness, enamel fracture and pain. It is irreversible.

It is ironic that those who aim to follow a healthy lifestyle can be putting their children at increased risk of tooth erosion. Eating acidic fruit between meals, consumption of fruit juices, particularly citrus fruit, and drinking fruit based teas can all increase erosion. Modern strains of apples, such as Fuji and Braeburn, have higher sugar levels than the more traditional strains of ten years ago, such as Granny Smith and Cox's Orange Pippin. As apples also have high acidity levels, confusion about the 'an apple a day' message is understandable. Healthy, but acidic, snacks such as yoghurt and pickles, also contribute to tooth erosion. Oral hygiene practices can also inadvertently worsen the situation because brushing teeth within an hour of exposure to acids, at the time when enamel has been softened, increases wear before the enamel has a chance to harden again.

Half of children between the ages of 4 to 18 now have tooth erosion with 5–12 per cent (depending on age) showing spread to the soft centre of the tooth (the dentine where the nerves are). It is thought that a large contributor to this is the 20 gallons of soft drinks per person drunk in the UK (though this still falls short of the 54 gallons per person drunk annually in the US – they also have higher tooth erosion levels).

Drinks that trigger dental erosion because of their acidity include fruit juices, fruit teas and colas. Some are worse than others, and, for instance, orange sodas are worse than colas. The phosphoric acid in sodas, by the way, is the same stuff in kettle descalers, so no wonder it eats teeth away. But what is most important is the frequency of intake of acidic drinks, how they are drunk and whether they are taken with meals or on their own. Cola sipped over 20 minutes and swilled around the mouth, as is often the habit, will do more damage than juice taken with a meal. Drinking acidic drinks through straws will lead to a characteristic 'notching' of front teeth. Eating stimulates saliva flow, and saliva buffers, or normalises, the altered acidity caused by these foods and drinks.

There are other causes of acid leading to tooth erosion, such as children's medicines, some iron tonics and chewable aspirin when taken long term, and soluble or chewable vitamin C (ascorbic acid) and other child-friendly chewable vitamins. And if your child is a frequent swimmer, beware of pools where the chlorine levels (and thus the acidity levels) are not properly controlled.

Ways of Preserving Dental Health

- Eat a diet rich in calcium, magnesium and vitamin C.
- Eat sweet treats with meals. It is the frequency of sugar and carbohydrate consumption, rather than the total intake, that is most detrimental to dental health.
- Consume acidic foods, such as fruits, yoghurts and pickles, and drinks such as fruit juice or carbonated drinks, mainly with meals.
- Rinse the mouth with water and avoiding brushing teeth for an hour after consuming an acidic food or drink.
- Avoid swilling acidic drinks around the mouth or sipping them slowly over time.
- Eat non-eroding snacks such as vegetable sticks with dips, toast with nut butter, a cube of cheese, nuts or crispbreads instead of fruit, and drinking water, sugar-less tea or milk instead of acidic drinks. (Tea naturally contains fluoride, which strengthens enamel).
- Chew sugar-free gum to encourage saliva flow two or three times daily after a meal. Saliva naturally 'buffers' the acids.

Tummy Trouble and Toilet Problems

As with any child's health problem your first port of call, to diagnose an acute digestive or bowel problem, is your doctor. This is to rule out any underlying serious problem that might need medical care. Some examples of these could be bacterial infections (including food poisoning), coeliac disease, an incompetent stomach sphincter or appendicitis. However, in a majority of cases the fundamental problem will be dietary and nutritional, or sometimes stress or emotional, and can be managed with a few small changes.

Bloating, Colic and Wind

Trapped wind can be extremely uncomfortable. It could be a sign of poor digestion or a food intolerance. Some measures to try include:

- The most likely food intolerance which leads to uncomfortable wind is to wheat-based products.
- Lactose intolerance is common in children and should be ruled out (*see* Milk and Dairy, page 162).
- Too much sugar or refined carbohydrates in the diet can feed 'bad' bacteria in the bowel leading to wind. Cut these out and also supplement with beneficial, child-formulated bacteria that include acidophilus and bifidobacteria.
- Other causes of wind, bloating and colicky symptoms are carbonated drinks.
- Teas which soothe include mint, slippery elm, fennel and aniseed.
- *See also* the information on Yeast Infections, page 245.

Constipation

Constipation can be very painful and lead to a child becoming frightened of going to the toilet. It is important to break this cycle. Set up a regular time of the day when your child sits on the toilet instead of waiting too long. Children often don't want to go to the toilet at school and establishing this routine can become important. Common causes of constipation in children are:

- An insufficient intake of fruits and vegetables.
- An insufficient liquid, and particularly water, intake.
- Repeat bouts of constipation in children are often related to food intolerance, particularly milk and other dairy products. Fairly often it can relate to to soya and wheat products.
- Very high fibre cereals designed for adults are not appropriate for children. Gentler options are porridge and ground up seeds. Linseeds, in particular, when added to cereals or yoghurts, are very successful at dealing with constipation – only a teaspoonful, or two at most, a day will be needed for a child.
- Slippery elm is a herb which can help.

Diarrhoea

This is most commonly a problem in relation to a bacterial or viral infection. Food poisoning should always be reported to your doctor. In small children diarrhoea can easily lead to dehydration (see Vomiting, page 244). Sometimes, diarrhoea can also be related to a parasite infestation, and this can be checked for by your doctor. Diarrhoea is often a sign of food intolerance and is frequently the other side of the coin to constipation (see above). Peppermint is an important herb to relieve bowel irritation. Another herb, tormentil, is used for diarrhoea and bowel inflammation as it sooths the digestive tract and provides a protective barrier against infective organisms. Another major cause of diarrhoea in children is taking a course of antibiotics. Always replace good bowel bacteria by taking probiotics (acidophilus and bifidobacteria) for 4–6 weeks after a bout of diarrhoea or after taking antibiotics. Child formulations are available and safe to take. Buy a product which guarantees live organisms and make sure it has been properly stored in the fridge by the shop and it is within its sell-by date. Prebiotics, which are the substrate or food which promote the growth of beneficial bowel bacteria, are also immensely useful. Both pre- and probiotics can be taken a few weeks before travelling to countries that are notorious for 'traveller's tummy' to reduce the risk of diarrhoea from food poisoning or contaminated water (though care should still be taken with food and water consumed). Nutrition Now make Rhino FOS and acidophilus for children which combines pre- and probiotics and is available by calling 0800 413 596.

Malabsorption

Some children have a compromised ability to absorb certain nutrients. In its most severe manifestation a problem like coeliac disease needs to be diagnosed by your doctor. In the worst cases this manifests as 'failure to thrive' where a child is simply not absorbing sufficient nutrients to grow properly. However, there are forms of sub-clinical malabsorption which your doctor will probably not be able to diagnose. For this it is best to see a paediatric nutritionist. In these cases some aspects of the diet are likely to be interfering with optimal absorption of nutrients, which is enough to show as symptoms such as wind and bloating, but not enough to manifest as failure to thrive. The most likely sensitivities are to wheat-based foods and then to other grains such as rye, oats and barley. Sometimes dairy products are also involved (see Food Intolerances, page 82, and Milk and Dairy, page 162). A nutritional therapist will then seek to repair the lining of the digestive tract using certain nutrients which are best used under supervision, particularly with children. At home, however, it is quite safe to increase essential fatty acid levels in a child's diet, or, using supplements, to help heal mucus membranes in the digestive tract. Borage oil has a high level of these beneficial oils. Alternatively, include a teaspoonful or two daily of flax oil in the diet by using it to dress salads or vegetables.

Tummy Ache

A tummy ache could be a sign of food intolerance, particularly if it recurs at specific times, say after eating a specific type of food or meal (*see* Bloating, Colic and Wind, page 241, for more on this). It can also be a sign of migraine (*see* Headaches, page 80). Peppermint tea relieves stomach ache very effectively. I would not generally suggest food combining for children but if tummy aches persist it may be worth a short course of two weeks food combining to see if it makes a difference. Food combining involves eating carbohydrates and proteins away from each other – so a meal would consist of, for example, meat and vegetables or rice and vegetables, but not of meat and rice together. If it is found that this brings relief consult a nutritional therapist for longer-term advice to ensure no nutritional deficiencies build up.

Vomiting

Projectile vomiting should always be taken seriously as it could be the sign of a serious infection. If food poisoning was contracted at a restaurant then this should be reported to your doctor who will notify the proper authorities. Severe vomiting can also lead to dehydration quite quickly in children and you should always consult your doctor or a pharmacist about rehydration. In children, vomiting can also be a sign of a migraine. For more on this, *see* Headaches, page 80. If the vomiting is a sign of food allergy then you should not attempt to reintroduce the food at a later stage as there might be a more serious reaction the next time around. Sometimes regurgitation is due to an incompetent sphincter and your doctor can advise on this. After a bout of nausea or vomiting avoid hard to digest foods, particularly milk and dairy foods, and avoid large meals. Instead offer soothing and easy to digest broths, soups, porridges (oats, rice), smoothies made with rice milk (*see* page 55 for ideas) and fresh non-acidic diluted juices.

Yeast Infections

Candida albicans, a yeast which causes yeast infections, for the most part lies dormant in the intestines in most people. Normally it does not do any harm. It is only when conditions are right that it gets out of control and proliferates causing unpleasant symptoms. A weakened immune system is one reason for it to get out of control, another is a diet which 'feeds' it. Perhaps the most common reason for it to turn nasty, however, is a course, or, more usually, repeated courses of antibiotics.

Yeast infections, or thrush, can cause mouth infections, nappy rash and vaginal or anal symptoms. If your child is itching 'down below' or has any white discharge then a correct diagnosis from a doctor is advisable. It is important to rule our urinary tract infections and other problems that can lead to further problems if left unchecked. When girls start menstruating, their hormone shifts can also trigger them into bouts of thrush.

From a dietary point of view, sugary foods and refined carbohydrates, including sugary cereals, canned drinks (including diet drinks) and white bread can make it worse. Alcohol is also a major factor (hopefully not relevant, though possibly in the case of a teenager).

Garlic is a potent antifungal and a half-clove should be included in food each day, as should cold-pressed olive oil, which can be used to dress salads. Take a multivitamin supplement daily but make sure it is yeast-free (B-vitamins are often derived from brewer's yeast). It is absolutely essential after a course of antibiotics to take a course of probiotic supplements, which include acidophilus and bifidobacteria, for at least a month, and ideally two months. This will help to keep an overgrowth of yeast from establishing itself. All of these measures are quite safe for children.

Vegetarians and Vegans

People are increasingly turning to vegetarianism for ethical and for health reasons.

Yet bringing up vegetarian children in our meat-eating society can mean parents are assaulted by opinions from friends and relatives who believe it is unwise for the health of a small child, or who worry that the child might feel different from his or her friends. Such worries are generally unfounded. It is perfectly possible to bring up a healthy vegetarian child, though it is also just as easy to bring up a junk-food vegetarian as it is a junk-food omnivore, if you are not careful. But you don't have to look far for positive role models. Many ethnic communities are vegetarian and have well-nourished children. These include Hindus, Jains, Seventh-Day Adventists and some Buddhists.

Of course, all children have specific nutritional needs that must be met whether they are vegetarian or omnivores. From weaning to toddlerhood is a time of rapid growth and this growth must be fuelled by building blocks (proteins), cement (vitamins and minerals) and construction energy (carbohydrates and body fat).

How Nutritionally Sound Is Vegetarianism?

Some people describe themselves as vegetarians but they eat fish, so technically they are 'fishitarians'. These diets are virtually identical, or superior, nutritionally speaking, to meat eaters' diets. A true vegetarian avoids meat, fish and fowl and their by-products, though they still eat eggs and/or dairy. From a nutritional viewpoint, these protein sources are easily replaced with plant sources of protein (*see* box). As a progression from vegetarianism, some people decide to become vegan. (This often occurs when they realise that dairy producers are a major supplier of calves for the meat industry, as a cow must be pregnant to produce milk and 50 per cent of calves are male.) Vegans avoid all animal products, including eggs and dairy, and sometimes honey. Vegan parents need to be careful to ensure their children's diet has enough calories and nutrients.

All children need a balanced diet and as long as they are getting the nutrients they need it doesn't matter if they are avoiding meat. Meat in the diet is an easy way of obtaining iron, zinc and vitamin B_{12}, which are needed for blood and brain function, growth and bone health. Oily fish provides vitamin D (as well as important fatty acids and selenium). Children who don't eat meat or dairy need two portions of protein food daily, such as peas, beans, lentils, other pulses, tofu, seeds and nuts. Ways to improve the vegetarian or vegan diet in the absence of meat include:

- Seed and nut butters are a useful standby and there are many soya-based products available.
- Serve a source of vitamin C, such as a small glass of orange juice, a piece of fruit or some broccoli with each meal. This

doubles the absorption of iron from non-meat sources.

- Fish can provide useful omega-3 fats for brain and immune health. Vegetarian sources of fats in the same family include flax and canola (rapeseed) oil, which can be added to dishes. Linseeds, walnuts and soya are other sources.
- Beans and lentils give valuable iron and zinc. Other good sources of iron are fortified cereals, dried fruit and bread, while nuts and seeds are good alternative sources of zinc.
- Yeast and specially fortified margarines and soya milk are sources of vitamin B_{12}.
- Soya is a valuable source of protein, but avoid giving too much. There is some concern that an excess in the diet might affect hormonal balance in small children. A modest portion three or four times a week should be fine.
- We get vitamin D from exposure to sunlight. In winter, or if your child is regularly covered up, fortified margarine and infant vitamin drops may be needed. Vitamin D deficiency is a problem in some ethnic groups who cover up from top to toe when out of doors and there has been a resurgence of rickets.
- As vegan diets are bulky and high in fibre but not necessarily very high in calories, include energy-rich nuts and seeds (nut and seed butters are handy), avocados, vegan margarines and soya products.

Signs that your toddler or child may be short on the nutrition they need include a failure to gain weight or height (check this against the centile charts provided by your health visitor) or if your child is pale or listless. An inability to concentrate might also be a sign to watch out for. If you are concerned about any aspect of your child's health you must check first with your doctor or health visitor (who can give you information on bringing up a vegetarian child) and then, if relevant, with a paediatric dietician or nutritionist.

Stocking a Vegetarian Cupboard

Vegetarian cooking does not require any special skills. Often it is simply a case of substituting one ingredient for another – for instance, making a Shepherdess pie (beans, mushrooms and vegetables in a rich tomato sauce with a potato crust) instead of a Shepherd's pie, or a vegetable-based spaghetti sauce rather than a meat-based one. Here are some foods for your pantry:

- Soya dairy alternatives: milk, cheese, yoghurt, cream, desserts.
- Quorn or soya mince to substitute for minced meat.
- Protein sources such as beans (baked, butter, flageolet, pinto, chickpeas), lentils (ideal for soups and casseroles) and tofu (available in a range of flavours and textures, such as dips, and for kebabs).
- Rice and pasta are good sources of energy, as are other dried grains such as oats, corn and millet. Also potatoes, yams and sweet potatoes.
- Dried fruit, apple sauce or juice, or maple syrup can all be used for sweetening.
- Vegetable stock cubes, bouillon or yeast extract (though all of these are too salty for babies). Tomato or garlic purées add lots of flavour.
- Whole nuts must be avoided by small children as there is a risk of choking. Nut products must also be avoided if there is any concern about allergy. However, from about one year ground nuts can be added to dishes such as pesto, nut butters (such as almond) can be used as spreads, and tahini (the sesame paste found in hummus) can be given too.
- If the vegetarian symbol appears on products they are vegetarian, the eggs are free-range and no GM ingredients are used.

What to Avoid

These are some hidden sources of animal products:

- All stock cubes other than vegetable.
- Worcestershire-style sauces, which can contain anchovies.
- Animal fats can be found in some pastries, cakes, biscuits and desserts – check the labels.
- Non-vegetarian cheese can contain animal rennet from calves' stomachs.
- Gelatine used in jellies and sweets. Products are available using non-animal gelling agents. Gelatine can also be found in drinks containing beta-carotene (though not in foods containing beta-carotene). Finings are often animal derived and used for getting rid of the cloudiness in apple juice. Check if juices are suitable for vegetarians.

At School and Beyond

You will need to pay particular attention on outings, visits to friends' houses, parties, stays at child minders and even school meal times to make sure that your child has sufficient non-animal source foods. You may already be well versed in how to handle these issues, but inevitably you will be caught out on occasion. Some people may just be dying to put a spoke in the wheel and serve foods you would not like your child to eat. It is important not to make your child feel responsible or guilty if this happens.

You will need to keep a regular, open dialogue about the issues in ways that are appropriate for each age. Questions are bound to arise on a regular basis. For instance, one particularly tricky situation to explain to your vegetarian child is why perfectly nice people, friends and relatives, eat animals when your family have decided not to. As your child grows he will develop a mind of his own and this may be at odds with your values or beliefs. This is only natural as a child aims to find their own identity. Your child may want to be one of the crowd and to not stand out or they may be rebelling. At some point you will need to decide that your child has the right to eat as he or she chooses. Many vegetarian parents talk to their children about the way they feel on these issues well ahead of time so that there is no misunderstanding later on. One compromise that seems to work successfully during 'rebellion' times is that if animal foods are eaten it does not happen in the home.

- Vegetarian Society 0161 925 2000 www.vegsoc.org
- Vegan Society 01424 427 393 www.vegansociety.com

Vitamins and Minerals

In an ideal world (if such a place exists) your child would be able to get all that he needs from his diet. The best way to achieve this is to eat a varied, mixed diet based on as many different types of foods as possible.

Intakes, Sources and Deficiencies

A varied diet ensures a good basic intake of the nutrients needed for growth and excellent health. Below are food sources of the nutrients that are important in childhood, with things to watch out for in case they may be deficient in your child's diet, such as erratic food fads, food processing and cooking methods.

Why Your Child Needs Certain Nutrients

Energy: vitamins B and C, iron, magnesium, iodine, chromium

Bone: calcium, magnesium, vitamins D and K

Growth and repair: zinc, B-vitamins and folic acid

Immunity: vitamin C, antioxidants, selenium and zinc, essential fatty acids

Brain: omega-3 fatty acids, B-vitamins, zinc, iron, selenium

Eye health: vitamin A, carotenoids (lutein and xeaxanthin), vitamin C

Lung health: carotenoids (beta-carotene), antioxidants (proanthocyanidins)

Antioxidants

All fruits and vegetables are rich in antioxidants and of particular use are the dark red/purple berries, such as cherries, blueberries and blackberries, which are a source of highly protective proanthocyanidins, and carotene-rich foods, such as carrots, cantaloupes, tomatoes, watermelon, apricots and green leafy vegetables (the green chlorophyll in leafy veg masks the carotene colours but they are there in abundance, such as lutein and xeaxanthin in spinach).

There are no recommended/reference intakes for the hundreds of different antioxidant nutrients, though it is recommended we consume five portions of fruit and veg daily. However, the average child eats only two or three portions daily. For a list of some of the sources, *see* Immune Boost, page 107.

Vitamin A

This is a fat-soluble vitamin, which is needed for healthy eyes and skin and is stored in the liver. As well as being found in fatty foods, it is also made in the body from beta-carotene, which comes from vegetables and fruits (*see* antioxidants above).

Vitamin A – RNI per day

1–6 years	400 mcg
7–10 years	500 mcg
11–14 years	600 mcg
15–18 years(m)	700 mcg
15–18 years (f)	600 mcg

Good sources of Vitamin A – mcg/portion

liver, 50 g	20,000
cod liver oil, 1 tsp, 5 ml	900
cheddar, 50 g	160
whole milk, 250 ml	150
cream cheese 30 g	130

egg, 1	110
butter/margarine, fortified, 10 g	83
herrings, 50 g	50
yoghurt, whole milk, 150 g	45

B-vitamins

These are water-soluble nutrients and they are vulnerable to depletion in foods as a result of long-term food storage, heat, light and cooking. For instance, chips you make from scratch have around 0.24 mg of thiamine (vitamin B_1) while frozen chips have 0.11 mg per 100g. Whole grains are the best sources, but if a child eats mainly white bread and white rice they may not be getting all they need. Many processed cereals have been fortified with the B-vitamins that were stripped out of them. Stress also increases the need for B-vitamins. In the charts below vitamin B_5 is omitted because there is not established RNI and it is generally available in a wide variety of foods.

B-vitamins – RNIs per day

	B_1	B_2	B_3	B_6	B_{12}	Folic Acid
	mg	mg	mg	mg	mcg	mcg
1–3 years	0.5	0.6	8	0.7	0.5	70
4–6 years	0.7	0.8	11	0.9	0.8	100
7–10 years	0.7	1.0	12	1.0	1.0	150
11–14 years (m)	0.9	1.2	15	1.2	1.2	200
11–14 years (f)	0.7	1.1	12	1.0	1.2	200
15–18 years (m)	1.1	1.3	18	1.5	1.5	200
15–18 years (f)	0.8	1.1	14	1.2	1.5	200

Good Sources of B-vitamins

Thiamine (Vitamin B_1) mg/100 g

quorn	36.6
Marmite	3.2
fortified cereals	1.0
branflakes	1.0
oats	0.9
pork chop	0.66
bacon, grilled	0.43
wholemeal bread	0.34
kidney	0.32
peas	0.26
liver	0.26
homemade chips	0.24
potatoes, boiled	0.18
lentils	0.11

Riboflavin (Vitamin B_2 mg/100 g)

Marmite	11.0
liver	4.4
fortified cereals	1.3
cheddar	0.40
eggs	0.35
mushrooms, cooked	0.34
beef	0.33
chicken, lean	0.19

Niacin[*] (Vitamin B_3) mg/100 g ([*] equivalent)

chicken, lean	8.2
pork chops	5.7
wheatgerm	4.5

wholemeal bread	4.1
beef	3.6
cod	1.7
white bread	1.7
potatoes	0.5

Vitamin B_6 mg/100 g

wheatgerm	3.3
cod	0.38
potatoes	0.33
turkey	0.32
beef	0.3
banana	0.29
chicken	0.26
Brussel sprouts	0.19
baked beans	0.14
wholemeal bread	0.12
yam	0.12
oranges	0.10
white bread	0.07

Vitamin B_{12} mcg/100 g

liver	81.0
liver pâté	7.2
eggs	2.5
beef	2.0
cod	2.0
fortified cereals	1.7
cheese	1.1
Marmite	0.5

Folic acid mcg/100 g

fortified cereals	250
legume beans	210
peanuts	110
Brussel sprouts	110
broccoli	64
lettuce	55
chickpeas	54
almonds	48
eggs	39
wholemeal bread	40
white bread	29
peas	26
potatoes	26

Vitamin C

This is an antioxidant nutrient, and is also used for skin repair and energy production. It is water soluble and is easily depleted by light, oxygen, storage and cooking. As well as citrus fruit, include kiwi, strawberries, blackcurrants, cabbage and broccoli in your diet.

Vitamin C – RNI

1–10 years	30 mg
11–14 years	35 mg
15–18 years	40 mg

Good Sources of Vitamin C – mg/100 g

blackcurrants	130
peppers, raw	120
strawberries	77
watercress	62
Brussel sprouts	60
kiwi	59
citrus	30–55
cabbage, raw	49
orange juice	39
mango	37
raspberries	32
cauliflower, cooked	27
branflakes	25
cabbage, cooked	20
potatoes	10–25
tomatoes	17
liver/kidney	10
beetroot	10

Vitamin D

Its main function is to help absorb calcium into bones and teeth. It is known as the 'sunshine vitamin' as our stores are built up in the spring and summer. Around 30 minutes out of doors per day is needed in the summer months. There are, however, serious deficiencies apparent in children from ethnic backgrounds whose cultures dictate that they stay covered up and as a result we are seeing a resurgence of rickets (bowed long bones of the legs). Darker skins need more exposure than lighter skins. There are, unfortunately, few food sources of vitamin D.

Vitamin D – RNIs

1–3 years	7.0 mcg
4–18 years	0*

*At risk groups (i.e. those not exposed to sunlight, such as invalids or those who remain covered up all the time) need dietary or supplemented vitamin D.

Good Sources of Vitamin D – mcg/100 g

cod liver oil	210.0
herring/kipper	25.0
salmon, canned	12.5
margarine, fortified	7.9
evaporated milk, unreconstituted	3.9
cornflakes, fortified	2.1
milk, skimmed, fortified	2.1
eggs	1.7
butter	0.8
liver	0.5
cheddar	0.3
milk, whole	0.03

Vitamin E

Vitamin E is an antioxidant nutrient and also helps keep blood thin. There is no RNI established for vitamin E, though it is known that some is essential in the diet and the estimated levels are around 3–4 mg daily for children.

Good Sources of Vitamin E – mg/100 g

wheatgerm oil, 1 tsp	9.0
almonds, shelled (25 g)	6.3
walnuts, shelled (25 g)	4.9
sunflower seeds, 1 tbsp	7.5
avocado, 1/2 pear	3.0
rice, brown, cooked (100 g)	2.0
tomatoes, two	1.8
chickpeas, cooked (100 g)	1.6
wholemeal bread, 2 slices	1.5
olive oil, 1 tsp	0.3
margarine, spread on 1 slice bread	0.8

Vitamin K

This is a fat-soluble vitamin needed for blood clotting and for bone health. It is made by the bowel flora, if there is a healthy balance. It is unlikely to be deficient in childhood and there is no RNI established (though it is injected as a matter of course into all newborn infants to prevent the risk of hemorrhagic disease).

Good Sources of Vitamin K – mcg/100 g

cauliflower, raw	3,600
liver	600
tomatoes	400
runner beans	290

soya beans, cooked	190
broccoli, cooked	175
cabbage, cooked	125
Brussel sprouts, cooked	100
potatoes, boiled	80
cheese, hard	50
meat*	50

* This is the average value of different types of meat

Essential fatty acids

There are two groups to which the essential fats belong, omega-6 and omega-3. In particular, the fatty acids found in the omega-3 group tend to be low in the UK diet, especially those found in oily fish. They are likely to be especially important for brain and immune health, and for controlling inflammatory diseases such as asthma. Good sources include oily fish, such as mackerel, sardines, salmon and tuna, fresh nuts, such as almonds and walnuts (grind and add to other dishes for small children) and cold-pressed seed oils. Most children who eat fish in the UK eat white fish, not oily fish.

There are concerns about pollution and oily fish with levels of PCBs and dioxins building up in fish. Mercury, a toxic metal, is also a hazard in some fish species. The official guidelines are that children should eat two portions of fish weekly, one white fish and one oily fish. This should be the right level to achieve the health benefits without overdoing the risk of pollutants. There are some conditions, however, such as asthma where higher levels of oily fish might be beneficial. It is not advised that children take cod liver oil supplements, though regular fish oil supplements are fine.

Calcium

Milk is an easy source of calcium but not all children drink milk due
to taste preferences or because it disagrees with them. In many societies calcium intake is well below that in the West without obvious
side effects, however other cultures also have other dietary and lifestyle
habits that probably do not exacerbate calcium loss from bones. They
are also often more physically active, which increases bone density.
Many foods are good sources of calcium but if a child does not eat
a varied diet then dairy products may well be needed. Calcium-
enriched dairy alternatives (soya products, rice milk, oat milk) are
other options. Calcium loss is increased by sugar, salt (the average
UK child has twice the amount recommended), phosphoric acid (in
very high quantities in fizzy drinks and a major source of calcium
loss) and low vegetable diets (which are consequently low in magnesium, which is needed in a good ratio for bone health) caffeine (colas,
tea/coffee, chocolate).

Calcium – RNIs

1–3 years	350 mg
4–6 years	450 mg
7–10 years	550 mg
11–18 years (m)	1000 mg
11–18 years (f)	800 mg

Good Sources of Calcium

whitebait/sprats 50 g	430 mg
cheddar/Edam 25 g	180 mg

milk 100 ml	175 mg
sardines 35 g	175 mg
tofu 60 g	150 mg
legume beans 100 g	128 mg
whole sesame seeds	
(i.e. dark tahini) 10 g	120 mg
figs 25 g	65 mg
orange, 1	60 mg
prawns 40 g	60 mg
salmon, canned 50 g	50 mg
molasses 10 g	50 mg
greens/spinach 25 g	45 mg
chickpeas 50 g	35 mg
bread, 1 slice	35 mg
broccoli 50 g	28 mg
almonds, 10	25 mg
milk chocolate 10 g	24 mg

Chromium

A high sugar diet will cause this nutrient to be excreted. Chromium is needed for GTF (glucose tolerance factor), which helps to regulate blood sugar. There is no RNI established. Good sources of chromium include brewer's yeast (best source), meat, wholegrains, nuts and beans/pulses.

Iron

Around one in four infants in some parts of the UK are deficient, and in thousands it is sufficiently deficient for them to be anaemic. Socially deprived toddlers are particularly vulnerable. Iron deficiency is the most common nutritional disorder in the UK and can have serious longer-term effects, including developmental delays, behavioural disturbances and tiredness among infants. Research shows that few parents are aware of the causes or risks of iron deficiency in childhood. Milk is low in iron and weaning infants on to milk instead of on to formula is a common cause.

Meat provides the most easily absorbed form of iron. Vegetarian diets which are not well-balanced can increase iron-deficiency, and to avoid this it is important to eat protein foods that compensate (*see* Vegetarians and Vegans, page 246). If your child is a vegetarian, give a portion of vitamin C-rich food with iron-rich foods to double absorption of iron from plant sources. When girls start to menstruate this is also a major contributor, especially with heavy blood loss, and women are much more likely than men to be anaemic.

Iron – RNIs

1–3 years	6.9 mg
4–6 years	6.1 mg
7–10 years	8.7 mg
11–18 years (m)	11.3 mg
11–18 years (f)	14.8 mg[*]

[*] May be insufficient in the case of high menstrual loss when supplementation may be needed.

Good Sources of Iron

The most absorbable form of iron is found in meats:

liver 50 g	4.4 mg

mussels 40 g	3.0 mg
beef 50 g	2.5 mg
sardines 35 g	1.5 mg
chicken, dark meat, 50 g	0.95 mg
chicken, light meat 50 g	0.3 mg

vegetable sources are not as well absorbed but, quantity-wise, provide most of our iron:

branflakes 30 g	6.0 mg
baked beans 200 g	3.0 mg
molasses 10 g	2 mg
chickpeas 50 g	1.75 mg
figs, 2	1.25 mg
dried apricots 25 g	1.2 mg
cocoa powder 10 g	1 mg
beetroot 25 g	0.3 mg
brown rice 50 g	0.25 mg
mushrooms, raw 25 g	0.2 mg

Magnesium

This is the core molecule at the heart of chlorophyll and so is found in every green vegetable. If your child does not eat a lot of these he may be one of the 25–50 per cent of children who are deficient in this important nutrient. Magnesium is used for 300 different body functions, including building healthy bones and energy production.

Magnesium – RNIs

1–3 years	85 mg
4–6 years	120 mg
7–10 years	200 mg
11–14 years	280 mg
15–18 years	300 mg

Good Sources of Magnesium

peanuts 50 g	95 mg
millet, cooked 50 g	60 mg
Weetabix, 2	50 mg
legume beans 100 g	50 mg
muesli 50 g	45 mg
wholemeal bread 50 g	38 mg
okra, boiled 50 g	28 mg
taco shells 25 g	26 mg
sardines in tomato sauce 50 g	25 mg
prawns 40 g	25 mg
brown rice, cooked 50 g	20 mg
white bread 50 g	12 mg
Brussel sprouts, boiled 50 g	7 mg

Selenium

This mineral has been depleted in the UK diet ever since we stopped sourcing our wheat from selenium-rich North America and switched to selenium-poor Europe. Selenium is important for immunity as it is at the core of an essential antioxidant enzyme, and for balanced moods. It is estimated that average intakes for adults are 30–40 mcg daily, around 50 per cent below the RNI for adults, and it must be assumed that this is the same for children.

Selenium – RNIs

1–3 years	15 mcg
4–6 years	20 mcg
7–10 years	30 mcg
11–14 years	45 mcg
15–18 years (m)	70 mcg
15–18 years (f)	60 mg

Good Sources of Selenium

brazil nuts, 2	40 mcg
cashews 25 g	18 mcg
fish, white, 50 g	15 mcg
molasses 10 g	14 mcg
clams 25 g	12 mcg
baked beans 200 g	4 mcg
chicken 50 g	4 mcg
mushrooms, cooked 25 g	3 mcg
white rice, cooked 50 g	2 mcg
cornflakes 50 g	1 mcg

Zinc

Levels of this nutrients are poor in the UK, with between 37–72 per cent of children (depending on the age group) not getting enough.

As zinc is needed for 200 different processes in the body, including all protein metabolism, growth and repair of tissues, as well as digestive enzymes, it easy to see how this can lead to health problems. Meat, fish, seafood, lentils, ground almonds, eggs, oats are all good sources. Zinc and iron are found in many of the same foods as they are sourced from protein-rich foods.

Zinc – RNIs

1–3 years	5.0 mg
4–6 years	6.5 mg
7–10 years	7.0 mg
11–14 years	9.0 mg
15–18 years (m)	9.5 mg
15–18 years (f)	7.0 mg

Good Sources of Zinc

oyster, 1	8 mg
popcorn 25 g	2 mg
All-Bran 30 g	2 mg
steak 50 g	1.7 mg
wholemeal bread, 2 slices	1.3 mg
muesli 50 g	1 mg
branflakes 30 g	1 mg
sardines 35 g	1 mg
sesame seeds 15 g	1 mg
walnuts, shelled 30 g	1 mg
cheddar 25 g	0.7 mg

| chickpeas 50 g | 0.5 mg |
| lentils 50 g | 0.5 mg |

See also Nutrition Needs, page 172, and Junk Food, page 116.

Water

Children are more prone to dehydration than adults because of their size and because they are often more active. Parents are advised to ensure that their children drink six to eight glasses of water each day. How much fluid children actually need largely depends upon how active they are and their physical build. They also, obviously, need more water when the weather is warm.

A drop of just 3 per cent in body fluids can seriously affect both mental and physical performance and results in a 10 per cent reduction in muscle strength. Children particularly need to increase their water intake if they are affected by poor concentration, constipation, diarrhoea, fever, headaches or dry skin conditions. A sure sign of dehydration is when urine is anything darker than a very pale straw colour. Strong smelling wee is another sign. Thirst is a poor indicator of dehydration because it is frequently a last resort signal – in other words, a person is already slightly dehydrated when they get thirsty.

Water is a solvent, and many nutritional minerals, such as magne-

sium, potassium and sodium, are dissolved in it. Up to 10 per cent
of a child's calcium intake can come from tap water in a hard water
area or from bottled mineral water. The calcium in tap water is believed
to be responsible for the slightly lower heart disease rates in hard
water areas.

The 'Water is Cool in School' campaign is bringing some interesting facts to our attention. As a result of the campaign, some schools
are now allowing children to bring their own, labelled, bottles of water
to school to drink during class times. If your child's school does not
currently have a policy on this you might want to explore the possibility with them.

- It has been found that 10 per cent of schools have no drinking
  water facilities at all.
- In the majority of the remaining schools, taps are only available
  in toilet areas (which are not necessarily sanitary), cloakrooms
  or outside, rather than in classrooms, corridors or canteens.
  Twenty-eight per cent have only one tap for the whole school.
- Provision of drinking cups is also poor.
- There appears to be a general lack of awareness amongst school
  staff of the importance of providing water to improve concentration.
- Continence problems in children, including daytime wetting,
  also usually responds well to regular fluid intake and easy access
  to toilets.
- For more information visit www.wateriscoolinschools.co.uk or
  call 0117 960 3060.

See also Drink to Health, page 51.

Wet Beds

About one in ten children are still bedwetting at the age of five, so nocturnal enuresis is a headache for many parents. One in 20 still bedwet at the age of seven. Unfortunately, the consequences can include lack of self-confidence, teasing and a reluctance to stay the night with friends. Enuresis is not just naughtiness but is defined as a medical condition, yet 80 per cent of parents do not know this.

Possible causes of bedwetting include urine production not slowing down at night due to a low level of vasopressin (the hormone which is responsible for reducing night-time production of urine) and difficulty waking to the sensation of a full bladder. It can also be a symptom of emotional upset (such as bullying at school, parental discord, a new sibling or moving house) and in a small number of cases it is linked to a physical problem in the urinary tract, which your doctor can diagnose or rule out.

There are many possible measures to help a child who is bedwetting. These include the practical (rubber undersheet) as well as behaviour modification and awareness (using damp-activated alarms to wake the child). A child must never be made to feel ashamed or guilty about bedwetting, and it is usually a transitional phase.

- There is a wealth of information available from organisations such as The Enuresis Society (ERIC) www.enuresis.org or 0117 960 3060.
- Other useful sites are www.bedwetting.co.uk or www.MyNight Owl.org

There are a few nutritional possibilities to think about. Children with restricted fluid intake during the daytime are at higher risk of bedwetting. This may sound back-to-front, but studies have shown that children who have free access to drinking water and bathroom facilities during the day, which is particularly relevant at school, have considerably fewer problems in this department. The water intake keeps their kidneys and urinary system working properly, and they learn to correctly regulate their bathroom habits. Unfortunately, the availability of water in many schools is dire and understanding of the need for children to be properly hydrated during the day is poor. As well as bedwetting, poor liquid intake is related to poor concentration and to reduced sports performance.

Having said this, it is also true that it can help to limit liquid intake in the two hours before bedtime. A child's bladder holds around a cup-and-a-half of liquid, and it is easy to drink this amount just before bed. This does not mean denying all drinks if thirsty, but not overdoing it either.

If your child is taking in caffeine in any quantity, for example from colas, tea, other drinks, chocolate, hot chocolate or medicines, this may be contributing to the problem as caffeine has a diuretic action. Finally, in a very few cases, enuresis could be linked to food intolerances and if all else fails you could try ruling out the main offenders: wheat, eggs, corn, milk and dairy foods and chocolate. Cut these out for a week to see if it helps, and then re-introduce one by one to see if any of them trigger the problem again.

See also Water, page 270.

X-tra Insurance — Supplements

Ideally, your child will be eating a vitamin- and mineral-rich diet which meets all, or most, of his or her needs. However, we live in times when this can be difficult, and certainly government studies tell us that the average child is not eating in this way. Children can certainly eat erratically, and sometimes the food choices they make are not the most nutritious. Having said this, popping a daily supplement does not make up for a poor diet, so if your child is not eating appropriately over a long period of time, a supplement will help but you need to tackle the diet as well. If you want to give your child a supplement these are some things to consider:

- A basic child-formulated vitamin and mineral supplement is all that most children will need. Make sure it is child-formulated to ensure that the doses are well within the safe upper-limits for children.
- Preferably give a supplement at meal times. Nutrients are

normally absorbed with food and this can help them work better. In particular, fat-soluble nutrients (vitamins A, D and E) need the presence of fat to facilitate absorption. Another good reason for giving them with meals is because the combination of sugar and citric acid found in many child-formulated supplements erodes teeth (the chewables are the worst) and taking them with a meal reduces this considerably (though I would prefer to choose those with sugar rather than those with artificial sweeteners, labelled sugar-free).

- Do not leave supplements lying around, and this goes for any supplements you are taking as well. As they are often formulated to appear to be like sweets a child may be tempted to sneak more than he should have. In particular, an overdose of iron can be dangerous.

- Iron supplements may be needed if you doctor diagnoses anaemia (symptoms are pale complexion and listlessness, though do not self-diagnose). A low-dose iron tonic which does not promote negative symptoms such as constipation is Spatone+(0800 7311 740 www.spatone.com), another is Ferrogreen(08450 606070).

- Fish oil supplements and evening primrose oil (or borage oil) supplements can be very useful for children. In particular, the benefits of fish oil supplements are equal to eating oily fish for a variety of symptoms, according to studies. If your child has asthma, eczema, allergies or behavioural problems you may definitely want to try some of these (*see* the relevant sections in this book). They can also be useful to bolster a diet which does not feature much oily fish or fresh nuts and seeds.

- If you believe your child to have any food intolerances it is extremely important that you ensure they still have a rounded diet. By cutting out a commonly eaten food there is always a chance that they will be missing out on a major source of a whole food group and will therefore miss out on certain nutrients. For more advice on this, *see* Food Intolerances, page 82.

It may well be a good idea to ensure your child takes a general multi-vitamin and mineral supplement.

- For advice on using vitamin and mineral supplements for children with specific health concerns it may be best to consult a nutritional therapist. Contact BANT (British Association of Nutritional Therapists) at www.bant.org.uk or by calling 0870 606 1284. NS3UK (Nutrition Services 3 UK) have nutritional therapists who work with children and can be contacted at www.ns3uk.co.uk or by calling 01344 360 033.

- Most supplemented herbs are formulated for adults. Tinctures will say what a child dose is for that herb, if appropriate. When giving herbs to children check to make sure that they are safe. It may be best to seek the advice of a medical herbalist. Contact the National Institute of Medical Herbalists at www.btinternet. com/-nimh/ or call 01392 426 022. Napiers Herbalists have an advice line staffed by qualified medical herbalists 0906 802 0117 (this is a chargeable line).

- Probiotic supplements, also known as beneficial bacteria, are safe to give a child, though a child with a serious milk allergy may have to avoid lacbacillus bacteria. The main concern is buying a supplement with live bacteria which will do some good. A good supplement is made by Biocare (www.biocare.co.uk or 0121 433 3727). Make sure that you buy from a shop with a good turnover to ensure freshness, use within the expiry date and keep in the fridge. You can also use a prebiotic supplement. As the name suggests, this is one that gives the growing 'substrate' for good bacteria and so promotes the growth of healthy bacteria in the gut. They are very effective. FOS (fructo-oligosaccharade) is the main one available and it is pleasantly sweet tasting, like sugar, though it is actually an indigestible type of fibre. In excess it can cause wind and bloating, but in small quantities is well tolerated and very useful. Nutrition Now make Rhino FOS and acidophilus for children which combines pre- and probiotics and is available by calling 0800 413 596.

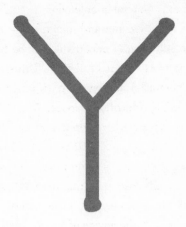

Young Helpers

Children love to be included. To do so requires an investment in time on your part, but if you are tempted to just get on with a task and exclude your child from being involved because you think it'll slow you down (which it probably will), this strategy may not serve you well in the long run. Whatever you are doing in the kitchen you can probably find an interesting job for them to do if they want to. Some ideas are:

- Shelling peas or chopping beans.
- Kneading dough or stirring mixtures.
- Cleaning out small stones from dried lentils and beans.
- Scrubbing potatoes or scraping carrots.
- Decorating biscuits or cakes.
- Collecting the ingredients for a recipe from the store cupboard.
- Checking things in the store cupboard to see if they are past their use-by dates.

- Weighing out ingredients.
- Finding recipes.
- Labelling boxes for the freezer.
- Watching the kettle boil (only joking – it never does!).

See also Projects and Activities, page 207, and Questions page, 210.